REVISE BTEC NATIONAL
Health and Social Care
UNIT 1

PRACTICE ASSESSMENTS Plus⁺

Series Consultant: Harry Smith
Author: Elizabeth Haworth

A note from the publisher

These practice assessments are designed to complement your revision and to help prepare you for the external assessment. They do not include all the content and skills needed for the complete course and have been written to help you practise what you have learned. They may not be representative of a real assessment.

While the publishers have made every attempt to ensure that advice on the qualification and its assessment is accurate, the official specification and associated assessment guidance materials are the only authoritative source of information and should always be referred to for definitive guidance.

This qualification is reviewed on a regular basis and may be updated in the future. Any such updates that affect the content of this book will be outlined at www.pearsonfe.co.uk/BTECchanges.

> **For the full range of Pearson revision titles across KS2, KS3, GCSE, Functional Skills, AS/A Level and BTEC visit:**
> www.pearsonschools.co.uk/revise

Published by Pearson Education Limited, 80 Strand, London, WC2R 0RL.

www.pearsonschoolsandfecolleges.co.uk

Copies of official specifications for all Pearson qualifications may be found on the website: www.qualifications.pearson.com

Text and illustrations © Pearson Education Ltd 2018

Typeset and illustrated by QBS Learning

Produced by QBS Learning

Cover illustration by Miriam Sturdee

First published 2018

21 20 19 18
10 9 8 7 6 5 4 3 2 1

British Library Cataloguing in Publication Data
A catalogue record for this book is available from the British Library

ISBN 978 1 292 25668 9

Printed in Slovakia by Neografia

Acknowledgement

The author and publisher would like to thank the following for permission to reproduce content:

P36 Springer Nature: Lu C, Xie M, Wendl MC, Wang J, McLellan MD, Leiserson MDM, Huang K, Wyczalkowski MA, Jayasinghe R, Banerjee T, Ning J, Tripathi P, Zhang Q, Niu B, Ye K, Schmidt HK, Fulton RS, McMichael JF, Batra P, Kandoth C, Bharadwaj M, Koboldt DC, Miller CA, Kanchi KL, Eldred JM, Larson DE, Welch JS, You M, Ozenberger BA, Govindan R, Walter MJ, Ellis MJ, Mardis ER, Graubert TA, Dipersio JF, Ley TJ, Wilson RK, Goodfellow PJ, Raphael BJ, Chen F, Johnson KJ, Parvin JD, Ding L. Patterns and functional implications of rare germline variants across 12 cancer types. Nature Communications. Dec. 22, 2015. www.nature.com/articles/ncomms10086   Material licensed under Creative Commons CC-BY 4.0

Note from the publisher

Pearson has robust editorial processes, including answer and fact checks, to ensure the accuracy of the content in this publication, and every effort is made to ensure this publication is free of errors. We are, however, only human, and occasionally errors do occur. Pearson is not liable for any misunderstandings that arise as a result of errors in this publication, but it is our priority to ensure that the content is accurate. If you spot an error, please do contact us at resourcescorrections@pearson.com so we can make sure it is corrected.

Websites

Pearson Education Limited is not responsible for the content of any external internet sites. It is essential for tutors to preview each website before using it in class so as to ensure that the URL is still accurate, relevant and appropriate. We suggest that tutors bookmark useful websites and consider enabling learners to access them through the school/college intranet.

Introduction

This book has been designed to help you to practise the skills you may need for the external assessment of BTEC National Health and Social Care – Unit 1: Human Lifespan Development. You may be studying this unit as part of the BTEC National Certificate, Extended Certificate, Foundation Diploma, Diploma or Extended Diploma in Health and Social Care.

About the practice assessments

The book contains four practice assessments for the unit, but, unlike your actual assessment, each question has targeted hints, guidance and support in the margin to help you understand how to tackle it.

 gives you relevant pages in the Pearson Revise BTEC National Health and Social Care Revision Guide so you can revise the essential content. This will also help you to understand how the essential content is applied to different contexts when assessed.

 gets you started and reminds you of the skills or knowledge you need to apply.

 helps you think about how to approach a question, such as making a brief plan.

 provides content that you need to learn such as a definition, rule or formula.

 reminds you of content related to the question to aid your revision on that topic.

 helps you avoid common pitfalls.

 appears in the final practice assessment and helps you become familiar with answering in a given time, and thinking about allocating appropriate time for different kinds of questions.

There is space within the book for you to write your answers to the questions. However, if you are planning or writing notes, or simply require more space to complete your answers, you may want to use separate paper.

There is also an answer section at the back of the book, so you can check your answers for each practice assessment.

Check the Pearson website

For overarching guidance on the official assessment outcomes and key terms used in your assessment, please refer to the specification on the Pearson website.

The practice questions, support and answers in this book are provided to help you to revise the essential content in the specification, and to help you review ways of applying your skills. The details of your actual assessment may change, so always make sure you are up to date on its format and requirements by asking your tutor, or checking the Pearson website, for the most up-to-date Sample Assessment Material, mark schemes and any past papers.

Contents

A small bit of small print

Pearson publishes Sample Assessment Material and the Specification on its website. This is the official content and this book should be used in conjunction with it. The questions have been written to help you test your knowledge and skills. Remember: the real assessment may not look like this.

Practice assessment 1

Revision Guide
page 5

> **Answer ALL questions.**
> **Write your answers in the spaces provided.**

All questions relate to one family.

1 | Samantha is 37 years old. She has three children. Emily is 12 years old, Belle is 5 years old and Lucas is 10 months old.

Describe what is meant by primary and secondary sexual characteristics giving **two** examples of each in relation to how Emily's body will change physically during puberty.

....

....

....

....

....

....

....

....

....

....

....

....

Total for Question 1 = 6 marks

Hint

For this **describe** question you need to include some detail rather than simply state a fact. You should write a definition of each of the two types of characteristics and for each one give two ways in which Emily's body will change.

Hint

Read the family information very carefully. The first part is given here and more information about the family will be added throughout this practice assessment. You will need to keep referring back to it as all the questions are based on specific family members.

Hint

Your answers must demonstrate that you are giving facts that are relevant to that specific person's age group and personal circumstances.

Watch out!

Remember that you are only being asked to give examples of **physical** changes to Emily's body.

Watch out!

No marks will be given for including examples that apply to boys.

Revision Guide
pages 1 and 5

Hint

In this **identify** question you need to simply state the fact asked for. You don't need to add any further detail.

Hint

Rate of growth means the speed at which Emily is growing. This question is asking you to say whether her rate of growth will stay the same, decrease or increase. (If you can't remember Emily's age, look back at the information given at the start of this practice assessment.)

Hint

When reading information from a graph it is useful to line your ruler up with the point on the graph being asked about, at right angles to either the horizontal or vertical axis. In this way, you can see what happens before and after that point more clearly.

Hint

This question is asking you to compare the rate at which Emily was growing before she was 12 with the rate at which she is expected to grow from now on. The point in the graph you are interested in is her height aged 12.

---

2 The graph shows how the average height of girls changes with age.

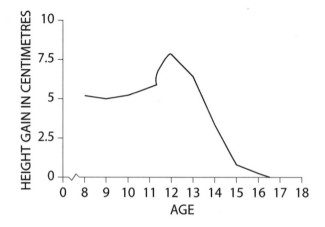

Identify what you would expect to happen to Emily's rate of growth over the next three years.

....

....

Total for Question 2 = 1 mark

3 | Belle is in reception class and her teacher tells Samantha she is developing as expected.

Explain **two** possible features of Belle's intellectual development at this stage of her life.

1 ....

....

....

....

2 ....

....

....

....

Total for Question 3 = 4 marks

Revision Guide
pages 9 and 12

Hint

For this **explain** question you need to name each feature and then add some detail to show that you understand the feature. For example, your first answer could be that she will ask lots of questions (the feature), which will satisfy her curiosity (the detail).

Hint

Refer back to the family information given at the start of this practice assessment, before Question 1, to check Belle's age.

Hint

You have only been asked for two features so choose the ones you know the most about.

Watch out!

Make sure you pick features that are relevant to Belle's age.

Revision Guide
pages 3 and 10

Hint

This **outline** question requires you to start by writing one sentence that outlines Piaget's theory.

Hint

Use the vocabulary about schemas provided in the flow diagram to help you answer this question properly.

Hint

Next you should outline an aspect of development that may be helped by crawling.

Hint

Finally, using the four stages of Piaget's theory, outline how this particular aspect will help Lucas to develop schemas.

Hint

There are many examples you can use to show how crawling helps a child develop schemas. For example, you could use Lucas's experience of crawling on different surfaces indoors or outdoors, which could be smooth, rough, slippery, solid, viscous, comfortable, less comfortable, of different temperatures, etc. Another example is bumping into different things.

4 Lucas is crawling.

Assimilation: the child constructs an understanding or concept (schema).

↓

Equilibrium: the child's experience fits with their schema.

↓

Disequilibrium: a new experience disturbs the child's schema.

↓

Accommodation: the child's understanding (schema) changes to take account of the new experience.

Piaget's schematic development theory

Outline what Piaget's theory explains about children. Then use his theory to give examples of how crawling will help Lucas's intellectual development.

....

....

....

....

....

....

....

....

....

....

....

....

Total for Question 4 = 6 marks

Revision Guide
page 13

5 Samantha has stayed at home to look after the children since Belle was born, but has been offered a job by a friend who is setting up her own business. She feels this is too good an opportunity to miss, so is going back to work next month. Her mother-in-law, Natalie, who is 60 years old and recently retired, will look after Lucas during the day and collect Belle from school.

Evaluate the development of Lucas's attachments during the infancy stage, with reference to the definition of attachment and the theories of attachment.

....

....

....

....

....

....

....

....

....

....

....

....

....

....

....

....

....

....

....

....

....

Total for Question 5 = 10 marks

Hint

In this **evaluate** question you need to draw on various sources of information, such as the family information and the theories of attachment, to consider positive and negative aspects of the situation.

LEARN IT!

Attachment is the emotional bond that is formed between infants and their main caregiver.

Hint

Give the definition to show you know what attachment means.

Hint

Check Lucas's age and refer to him by name.

Hint

Refer to Bowlby's theory about the importance of forming a strong attachment with the child's main caregiver.

Hint

Explain how the bond between Lucas and Samantha has developed since he was born (refer to Schaffer and Emerson's stages of attachment).

Hint

Write about how Lucas might react when Samantha starts to leave him and how his attachment to Natalie will develop.

Revision Guide
pages 21 and 31

Hint

In this **discuss** question you need to write in some detail about different aspects of Robert's life, how they might affect him and the extent to which they are important.

Prepare

Underline or highlight details in the information which will help you to answer the question. For example, we know that Robert has a wife and three children – might this be a contributory factor?

Hint

Present your answer so that it is clear and well organised, in a logical order considering each aspect in turn, looking at how it might have led to Robert's medical issues.

LEARN IT!

Genetic predisposition is an increased likelihood of developing a particular disease based on a person's inherited genes.

6 Samantha's husband, Robert, is 40 and loves swimming. He swims lengths of the local pool before work every day, and travels around the country taking part in extreme swimming races in rivers or the sea most weekends. He is very competitive. Robert is always hungry and finds he can eat what he wants and not put on any weight, due to his excessive exercise regime. He eats lots of pasta for energy, often in a creamy sauce, he snacks on biscuits throughout the day and, at weekends, often picks up takeaway meals for them all after a race.

During one race he starts to experience pains in his chest. Medical investigations show that he has had a heart attack and needs a surgical procedure on his heart, because of an undetected heart condition which may be due to genetic predisposition. His father died of a heart attack at the age of 50 and his mother, who is of South Asian origin, takes medication for high blood pressure. Blood tests also reveal that Robert is very close to developing diabetes, a condition where blood sugar is too high.

Using the information given about Robert and your own knowledge, discuss how **both** genetic factors **and** his lifestyle choices may account for Robert's medical issues.

....

....

....

....

....

....

....

....

....

....

....

....

....

....

....

....

....

....

....

....

....

....

....

Total for Question 6 = 10 marks

Explore

Research has shown that people of African-Caribbean and South Asian origin are much more likely to have high blood pressure than other ethnic groups in the UK. Those of South Asian origin are up to six times more likely to develop type 2 diabetes: this can further increase the risk of developing high blood pressure or having a heart attack. More information can be found on the website for the British Heart Foundation.

Revision Guide
page 30

Hint

For this **evaluate** question you need to draw on the family information and your own knowledge to consider both positive and negative aspects of the situation. Think about how Robert might react to finding he has these health issues. Depending on how he reacts, how will family life be affected?

Prepare

Underline or highlight significant new information which will help you to prepare your answer. Write down your initial thoughts, making connections between the facts and their potential impact on the rest of the family. (You could do this on a separate piece of paper.) This will also help you to structure your answer logically.

Watch out!

Remember this question is about the development of **the rest of the family** and not Robert. If you talk about Robert's mood, for example, say how this affects the development of the rest of the family.

Hint

You need to finish your evaluation with a conclusion of how you think Robert's issues will affect the development of the rest of the family overall, based on the facts you have included in your answer.

7 Robert has a major operation to remedy his heart condition and is advised to rest for a few weeks. He will then need to attend a heart clinic for a number of weeks, where he will undertake supervised exercise while wearing a heart monitor. He has also been told to avoid swimming or work until the cardiac specialist gives him permission, to go for short walks when he feels ready and to change his diet to reduce his blood sugar levels.

Evaluate the likely effects of the diagnosis of Robert's health issues on the development of the rest of the family.

....

....

....

....

....

....

....

....

....

....

....

....

....

....

....

....

....

....

....

....

Total for Question 7 = 10 marks

8 Robert is self-employed, running his own business from rented premises. Being unable to work for a few months puts a strain on the family finances. Samantha had only been at her new job for a few weeks when Robert became ill. After taking time off to help Robert through his initial recovery Samantha returns to work, leaving her mother-in-law to look after Lucas, but because her friend's business is only just starting to grow Samantha is not earning much.

Outline the ways in which the family's reduced income might affect Emily's intellectual development.

....

....

....

....

....

....

....

....

....

....

....

....

Total for Question 8 = 6 marks

Revision Guide
pages 9 and 28

Hint

This **outline** question is asking you to give an overview or summary of the ways in which the family's reduced income might affect Emily's intellectual development. Remember to include positive and negative points, so your answer is balanced and considered.

Hint

Make sure you check the family information at the start of this practice assessment to remind yourself of Emily's age before you start to answer.

Watch out!

Notice the focus of this question – it is about Emily's **intellectual** development, so you should not mention her physical, emotional or social development.

Watch out!

Don't be tempted to write about the effect on any other members of the family. It won't gain you any marks.

Revision Guide
page 28

Watch out!

You only need to **outline** the likely effects on Samantha's **emotional** health; it's important to notice the focus of a question and, in this case, it is only her emotional health you should focus on.

Hint

Make sure you read back through the various sections of family information, so you don't miss an important point. For example, Samantha has only recently started work after being at home since Belle was born – how might she feel when she is at work?

Hint

Although Samantha is enjoying being back at work there may still be some negative effects of this on her emotional health.

---

9 | Despite her worries about their financial position, Samantha really enjoys being back at work.

Outline how Samantha's enjoyment of her job may affect her emotional health.

....

....

....

....

....

....

....

....

....

....

....

....

Total for Question 9 = 6 marks

10 Samantha's grandmother, Joan, is 78 years old and lives with her husband, Fred, 73 years old, in sheltered accommodation. They moved there five years ago, leaving the house they had lived in for their whole married life after Fred suffered a stroke which left him with reduced mobility. He spent almost a year in hospital, first on a medical ward and then in the rehabilitation unit. He eventually regained his speech and most of his mobility and was able to return home, walking with the aid of a stick, but could no longer drive or play bowls. After Fred's return home from hospital, Samantha and Robert helped as much as they could but Joan had to do most of the cooking, washing, ironing and shopping, as well as helping Fred with his day-to-day needs. Fred's friend used to pick him up every week to take him to the pub, where they were part of a quiz team. He really enjoyed seeing his friends, taking part in the quiz and having a few pints of beer once a week.

Fred and Joan had both always enjoyed crossword puzzles and watching TV quizzes, trying to answer the questions before the contestants. Fred noticed that Joan was starting to forget things and getting so frustrated that she no longer wanted to pursue these hobbies and stopped watching TV. She then started to forget the names of everyday things and after a few months started to muddle the names of family members. Samantha took her to see their GP and she was diagnosed with Alzheimer's disease. Fred found it very distressing to see how quickly Joan's condition worsened and started to smoke again, a habit he had stopped 30 years ago because his family disliked it so much. Joan became increasingly forgetful and was often quite agitated. Samantha helped as much as she could but struggled to be there as often as she would have liked, due to her family and work commitments.

Fred did not keep up with his exercises after he had recovered as fully as he could from his stroke, and he now realises how important it is that he remains as mobile as possible to try to look after Joan and the house. Joan has good days when she can potter about and do a few jobs, but she doesn't like going out any more as she gets confused, and distressed, very easily. She is still in the early stages of Alzheimer's disease, but she is happiest at home seeing only close family members.

Fred now rarely goes out of the house except to sit on the patio of their small garden, when the weather allows. He is able to chat with his neighbours when he is out in the garden. He misses going to the pub with his friend but feels he needs to be at home to look after Joan, so he will have a few cans of beer after she is in bed a couple of times a week. He doesn't drink to excess though, as he needs to be alert in case Joan needs him in the night. The doctor has said that Fred will need to think about placing Joan in a residential nursing home when her condition reaches its final stage. Fred is adamant that he wants Joan to stay at home with him as long as possible, where he can look after her and be with her, as they haven't been apart since they married 52 years ago except during his stay in hospital.

Revision Guide
pages 35 and 39

Hint

In this **identify** question you need to simply list the correct number of the services asked for.

Hint

Re-read the information on the previous page, selecting the sections that are relevant, and referencing them in your answer.

Watch out!

This question is about Joan's Alzheimer's disease, and not about Fred.

Explore

Alzheimer's disease is a progressive disease with more parts of the brain being damaged over time. Proteins called plaques and tangles build up in the brain, leading to a shortage of chemicals, which affects the transmission of signals.

Identify **three** of the services that will be available to support Joan through the early stages of Alzheimer's disease.

1 ....

....

2 ....

....

3 ....

....

Total for Question 10 = 3 marks

11 Fred has suffered several major changes in his life over the past five years.

To what extent might recent life changes have affected Fred's social wellbeing?

....

....

....

....

....

....

....

....

....

....

....

....

....

....

....

....

....

....

....

....

....

....

....

Total for Question 11 = 12 marks

Revision Guide
pages 29, 30 and 37

Hint

For this **to what extent** question you need to give reasons from the case study to support your opinion as to how the life changes Fred has experienced will have affected his social development. Remember to mention the life changes you are referring to.

Prepare

Go back to the information about Fred and underline or highlight the relevant details which will help you to answer the question. Before you begin to write, plan your writing; for example, a spider diagram could help you to organise your thoughts. (You could draw this on a separate piece of paper.)

Watch out!

Remember that this question is about Fred's social wellbeing **not** his emotional wellbeing.

Hint

You need to construct a well-balanced, logical and clear argument, giving both positive and negative points.

Hint

Finish with a conclusion supported by the evidence given in the scenario.

Revision Guide
page 38

Think carefully about
Fred's new role in life
when considering how
activity theory applies to
Fred's recent life. It is to
look after Joan, not to
attend an exercise class.

Hint

As this question asks about
activity theory you need
to make it clear that you
understand it. You can do
this best by explaining what
activity theory says and
then applying it to the two
examples you pick. Make
sure you use words from
the theory accurately.

Hint

In your answer you will
need to refer to Fred's
new role in life and his new
interest.

Explore

Another question might
ask you to think about
how social disengagement
theory could be applied
to a case study based
on an elderly person who
has withdrawn from social
contact.

12 Fred wants to take up a new interest that will also help him look after
Joan. Samantha arranges for Emily to sit with Joan once a week, so
Fred can join an exercise class at the hospital for older people with
limited mobility. He finds it hard at first, but gives up smoking again,
and starts to enjoy the exercise, loses a little weight and makes new
friends.

With reference to the scenario, explain **two** examples of how activity
theory applies to Fred's recent life.

1 ....

....

....

....

....

....

2 ....

....

....

....

....

....

Total for Question 12 = 6 marks

13 Justify how giving up smoking will impact on Fred's health and wellbeing.

....

....

....

....

....

....

....

....

....

....

....

....

....

....

....

....

....

....

....

....

....

....

....

Total for Question 13 = 10 marks

TOTAL FOR PAPER = 90 MARKS

Revision Guide
pages 31 and 36

Hint

For a **justify** question you need to give reasons to support an opinion, so in this case you need to explain **how** you think giving up smoking will **improve** Fred's health and wellbeing **overall**. Make sure you include both positive and negative points.

Hint

Remember that health and wellbeing applies to Fred's physical, intellectual, emotional and social needs.

Watch out!

This question is about smoking so if you talk about other factors, such as exercising or losing weight, make sure you relate them to smoking.

Hint

Always use formal terms and avoid slang. For example, don't refer to 'cigs' or 'fags', but instead refer to cigarettes.

Hint

Remember to round off your answer with a short conclusion.

Revision Guide
page 7

Hint

In this **identify** question you simply need to state two symptoms of the menopause without any added detail.

Revision Guide
page 15

Hint

For this **outline** question you need to give a brief description of what parallel play is, then what cooperative play is.

Practice assessment 2

Answer ALL questions.
Write your answers in the spaces provided.

1 (a) Identify **two** symptoms of the menopause.

1 ....

....

2 ....

....

2 marks

(b) Briefly outline the key difference between parallel play and cooperative play.

....

....

....

....

2 marks

Sean is 42 years old and his wife, Caitlyn, is 39. They live with their twin boys, Aidan and Bowie, who are 8 years old, and Sean's daughter from a previous relationship, Mollie, who is 16 years old.

(c) Sean is in early adulthood. Describe **two** possible physical effects as he moves into middle adulthood and then starts later adulthood.

1 ....

....

....

2 ....

....

....

4 marks

Hint

The command word **describe** means that for each of the **two** physical effects you pick you need to say what they are and why each happens.

Hint

You can describe one effect from each of the two life stages mentioned or two from one life stage of your choice. Just remember to state which stage you are referring to and that they must be physical effects.

Hint

You need to show that you know that Sean is at his physical peak in early adulthood.

Watch out!

If you simply write down two physical effects you will only get a mark for each as you will have identified them rather than described them.

Revision Guide
pages 9, 10, 11
and 12

Hint

For this **describe** question
you need to state two
things the twins could do
when they were five years
old, such as use simple
sentences, and then, for
each thing, say how that
ability will have developed
by the time they are
aged 8.

Hint

Developing normally means
that they are developing
in the same way as an
average child of that age
will develop.

Hint

To answer this question
think about what you have
learned about intellectual
milestones and stages of
language development.
There are several different
answers you could give.

Aidan and Bowie are at primary school and are developing normally.

(d) Describe **two** ways in which their cognitive ability has changed since
they were 5 years old. They are now 8 years old.

1 ....

   ....

2 ....

   ....

4 marks

Aidan and Bowie are in early childhood and will most likely start puberty between the ages of 13 and 15 years.

(e) Explain how Aidan and Bowie will develop physically as they move from early childhood to adolescence.

....

....

....

....

....

....

....

....

....

....

....

6 marks

Revision Guide
page 5

Hint

For this **explain** question you need to say how Aidan and Bowie's bodies will change and why.

Hint

The reason why the boys' bodies will develop is because of changes in hormones, mostly an increase in testosterone. Therefore, you could start your answer by stating that, and then give at least six body changes this causes.

Hint

Make sure you use correct terminology rather than slang. For example, use 'penis' rather than any other word.

Watch out!

Be careful to restrict your answer to an explanation of physical changes to male bodies.

Revision Guide
pages 14, 16,
17 and 26

Hint

For this **discuss** question you need to consider different aspects of Mollie's possible development at college. To show that you are doing this thoroughly, it is important to give both positive and negative ways in which Mollie may develop.

Prepare

Think about how life in sixth-form college might be different to life in school. This should give you some ideas to write about.

Hint

To make sure you get a high mark you could try to think about one positive example for how Mollie might develop for each area of development, i.e. physical, intellectual, emotional and social, and then do the same with negative examples for each area.

Mollie is leaving school to start her BTEC Level 3 at the local sixth-form college.

(f) Discuss how moving to sixth-form college may affect Mollie's development.

....

....

....

....

....

....

....

....

....

....

....

6 marks

Caitlyn gave up her job in a busy office when she had the twins and returned to a similar job when the boys were settled in primary school.

(g) Describe **three** potential effects of Caitlyn's return to work on her social and emotional development.

1 ....

....

....

....

2 ....

....

....

....

3 ....

....

....

....

6 marks

Total for Question 1 = 30 marks

Revision Guide
pages 14, 16
and 17

Hint

The command word is **describe** so rather than just say, for example, 'she will be happier', you must also say **why** she will be happier.

Hint

Make sure you include at least three aspects of both social and emotional development in order to get high marks.

Hint

Remember that returning to work could have both negative and positive effects on Caitlyn.

Revision Guide
page 20

Hint

In this **discuss** question aim to include at least three ways in which nature plays a role in human development and at least three ways in which nurture plays a role in human development. This will ensure you give a balanced and full answer.

Hint

This question is a general one and does not refer to any of the case study material provided so far. This means that you don't need to link your answers to any of the people mentioned in this practice assessment and can answer the question in general terms.

LEARN IT!

Nature means the influence of inherited features on development.

Nurture means the influence of the environment a child is born into and brought up in on development.

Both nature and nurture play a part in human development.

---

2 (a) Discuss how nature and nurture both play a role in human development.

....

....

....

....

....

....

....

....

....

....

....

6 marks

(b) Evaluate the impact of bullying on the short- and long-term development of a child.

....

....

....

....

....

....

....

....

....

....

....

....

....

....

....

....

....

....

....

....

....

....

....

....

....

....

10 marks

Total for Question 2 = 16 marks

Revision Guide
page 26

Prepare

On a separate piece of paper draw a mind map to show all the effects that bullying may have on a child, including both short- and long-term effects. If you make any notes on the actual exam paper remember to cross them out if you don't want them to affect your marks.

Hint

In this **evaluate** question you need to look at different potential effects of bullying and decide how a combination of these will affect the development of the child being bullied in both the short and the long term.

Hint

Try to include a balance of short- and long-term effects. However, if you feel more confident writing about, for example, short-term effects, it is fine to include more of those.

Hint

Remember to finish with a conclusion which sums up your opinion.

Hint

This is a general question with no reference made to any case study material provided so far. You need to answer it in general terms and don't need to refer to any person described in this practice assessment.

Prepare

Underline or highlight relevant information in the case study which will help you to answer the question. For example, Martha's home environment may be an important factor to consider, or the length of time she has spent caring for Tavi.

Hint

For this **explain** question you need to not only state the effect but also include more detail. One possible answer is 'Martha will have a close relationship with Tavi because she spends so much time with him'. The second half of the sentence, from the word 'because' onwards, is what makes the difference between identifying an effect and explaining an effect.

Hint

There will be positive effects of looking after Tavi as well as negative, so it is important to include some of each, and to include at least six altogether to gain a high mark.

Hint

Remember that the question is about Martha and her health and wellbeing. There are no marks for writing about Tavi's health and wellbeing.

3 Adlai, aged 55, and Martha, aged 53, live in a large house with a big garden on the outskirts of a pretty village. Their son, Tavi, is 25 years old and is severely physically disabled. He can't work and lives at home, depending on his parents to help him with day-to-day tasks. Adlai has a well-paid job but Martha has not worked since Tavi was born. Tavi's sister, Bethia, is 20 years old. She is at university over 100 miles away and comes home for the holidays.

(a) Explain the likely effects of looking after Tavi for the past 25 years on Martha's health and wellbeing.

....

....

....

....

....

....

....

....

....

....

....

6 marks

Bethia graduates when she is 21 years old but is unable to find a suitable job straight away so returns home to live while she continues to apply for jobs.

Revision Guide
pages 14, 16, 17, 29 and 30

(b) Explain the possible effects on Bethia when she finds herself living at home again.

....

....

....

....

....

....

....

....

....

....

....

6 marks

Hint

For this **explain** question you need to give reasons to support your opinion of the possible effects on Bethia.

Hint

Remember that Bethia will have mixed feelings about living at home again, even though it is only until she can get a job which uses her talents and the knowledge and skills she has gained at university. Even her feelings about Tavi will be complicated, possibly ranging from love, to sadness, to resentment and to guilt.

Hint

There are many possible answers to this question but, to focus your response, try to think of a balance of positive and negative effects. Three of each will help you get a high mark.

Revision Guide
page 28

Hint

In this **justify** question you need to provide a summary of the impact on Bethia's health and wellbeing of her getting a suitable job. You must give both positive and negative effects.

Hint

It is a good idea to include a mixture of negative and positive points, covering each of Bethia's PIES needs, in order to gain good marks.

LEARN IT!

PIES = Physical, Intellectual, Emotional and Social needs.

Hint

You should finish the answer with your conclusion about whether getting the job will have an overall positive or negative effect, and why, on Bethia's health and wellbeing.

(c) Justify how getting a job which uses the skills and knowledge she gained doing her degree may impact on Bethia's health and wellbeing.

....

....

....

....

....

....

....

....

....

....

....

6 marks

(d) To what extent will Bethia getting a job and moving away from home permanently affect Tavi's social and emotional development?

....

....

....

....

....

....

....

....

....

....

....

....

....

....

....

....

....

....

....

....

....

....

....

....

....

....

10 marks

Total for Question 3 = 28 marks

Revision Guide
pages 14, 16 and 17

Hint

For this **to what extent** question you need to state clearly the reasons to support your overall view or opinion.

Hint

You need a mixture of positive and negative effects on Tavi's social and emotional development. Then say whether the overall impact is positive or negative, in order to gain a high mark.

Hint

You could start by writing some positive points, using starts of sentences such as 'Tavi may enjoy...' or 'Tavi may value...'. Then move on to negative effects, such as 'Tavi may feel frustrated because...' or 'Tavi may find it hard because...'.

Hint

Your answer should conclude with a summary of your overall opinion of whether the effect on Tavi's social and emotional development will be positive or negative, depending on the balance of the answers you have given.

Watch out!

Remember that your answer must focus on Tavi's social and emotional development, not Bethia's.

Revision Guide
page 30

Hint

In this **explain** question you need to state each effect and then add some detail, such as how it makes Arthur feel.

Hint

The information provided suggests that Arthur will miss Barbara very much. Therefore, it is not necessary to spend much time thinking about lots of positive effects as there will not be many. However, there will be lots of negative effects.

Explore

Spend some time thinking how different your answer would be if the question said that Barbara and Arthur had been unhappily married. Would there still be both positive and negative effects?

4 Arthur is 93 years old. He is mobile, only using a walking stick when he goes outside, and has lived in sheltered accommodation since his wife, Barbara, died two years ago, after being happily married for 71 years. He has two children, and four grown-up grandchildren, who live in different parts of the country. They take it in turns to visit him, so he sees a family member about once a fortnight. He has his own self-contained unit, with a living room, kitchen and wet room. If he needs help in an emergency, Arthur only has to press the personal alarm he wears around his neck and someone will come to check on him.

(a) Explain the possible effects of losing Barbara on Arthur's health and wellbeing.

....

....

....

....

....

....

....

....

....

....

....

....

6 marks

(b) With reference to the relevant theories of ageing, evaluate how support services could help Arthur to deal with the changes in his life.

....

....

....

....

....

....

....

....

....

....

....

....

....

....

....

....

....

....

....

....

....

....

10 marks

Total for Question 4 = 16 marks

TOTAL FOR PAPER = 90 MARKS

Revision Guide
pages 24, 38 and 39

Hint

For this **evaluate** question you need to consider what you know about Arthur to decide how support services might be able to help him.

Prepare

Refer to your notes to remind yourself of the facts about the relevant theories, which are the social disengagement theory and the activity theory. Write a bullet list of points you want to include in your answer.

Hint

Remember that you need to show your knowledge of the two relevant theories — then, for each one, say how relevant support services can help Arthur. To gain high marks you should write about each theory then give at least four examples for each.

Hint

The examples you give must show that you understand the theories. Any examples for the activity theory will be concerned with ways in which Arthur can access more social activities. However, those for the social disengagement theory must be to help him cope with his grief and his practical problems to give him contentment and allow him to reflect on his previous life and activities.

Revision Guide
page 4

Hint

For this **identify** question you need to simply provide the facts asked for. In this case you need to give the name of the fine motor skill relevant to a child aged 3 and give one correct example of the skill.

Hint

Think about the name of the motor skill and what new things this will enable Ben to do.

Hint

Previously Ben will have only been able to use a pincer or palm grasp.

Practice assessment 3

> **Answer ALL questions.**
> **Write your answers in the spaces provided.**

1   Leanne is 25 years old and lives with her partner, Dave, also 25 years old, and their 3-year-old son, Ben. Leanne's parents, Clare and Tony, divorced when she was 5 years old and her father moved to a different part of the country. Her mother, Clare, is suffering from cancer. Her grandfather, Peter, who is 70 years old, lost his wife 20 years ago and can no longer live on his own, so he now lives with Leanne and Dave.

(a) Ben is developing normally for his age. Identify **one** fine motor skill he will now be developing and **one** example of what this will enable him to do.

....

....

....

....

2 marks

(b) Identify **four** predictable life events Ben will experience during his childhood and adolescence.

1 ....

....

2 ....

....

3 ....

....

4 ....

....

4 marks

Revision Guide
page 29

Hint

To answer this **identify** question you need to state four predictable (expected) life events relevant to childhood or adolescence.

Hint

Remember to stick to predictable events that will happen to Ben during his childhood or adolescence. Answers relating to unpredictable events will not gain any marks.

LEARN IT!

Life events are also known as **transitions**.

Revision Guide
page 13

Hint

For this **explain** question you need to show that you understand what the question is about by including some detail in your answers.

Hint

The number of marks available should guide you on the amount of detail to include in your answer. Here, you need to write about **two** ways in which each of the **two** children is likely to behave when their mothers are still present, leave them or return for them.

Hint

Use Ainsworth's Strange Situation classification to answer this question.

Leanne is Ben's main caregiver and Ben has formed a secure attachment with her. Ben now attends nursery three times a week. Another child at nursery, Ollie, has an insecure, avoidant attachment with his mother who often rejects him because she has problems of her own.

(c) Using Ainsworth's Strange Situation classification, explain the difference between Ben's likely behaviour when Leanne takes him into nursery, leaves him and collects him, and Ollie's behaviour in the same situation.

....

....

....

....

....

....

....

....

4 marks

(d) Describe the differences between how Piaget believed children develop logic and reasoning and how his critics think this happens.

....

....

....

....

....

....

....

....

4 marks

Revision Guide
pages 10 and 11

Hint

For this **describe** question you need to write about one thing Piaget believed about children's cognitive development. You then need to say how his critics think differently about that same point. Then repeat this process to write a full answer.

Hint

The fact that the question is only worth 4 marks tells you that you do not need to include in-depth details such as Piaget's schematic theory, conservationism or egocentrism.

Hint

This question is a general one and does not refer to any of the case study material provided so far. This means that you don't need to link your answers to any of the people mentioned in this practice assessment and can answer the question in general terms.

Revision Guide
pages 9 and 32

Hint

For this **explain** question you need to say what Dave has learned about life, how this affects his thinking and how this will change as he passes from early to middle then later adulthood.

Hint

Your answer should include at least six facts, and should include at least one from middle adulthood and one from later adulthood.

Hint

Think about how physical factors such as diet and lifestyle will affect Dave's brain cells, and therefore his intellectual development.

Dave went to college then university after leaving school and is now an engineer.

(e) Explain how Dave's intellectual development changes as he passes through the three adult life stages.

....

....

....

....

....

....

....

....

....

....

....

....

6 marks

Leanne has always enjoyed exercise, being a dancer, and was very interested in any sports available to her while she was at school and university. She struggled to keep fit when Ben was born as she found looking after a baby very tiring, especially as her weight had increased by 10 kg. However, she is determined to reach full fitness again and intends to go for a run at least three times a week, while Ben is at nursery. She has also signed up for dance classes a couple of evenings a week, while Dave and/or Peter babysit.

(f) Evaluate the likely impact of exercise on Leanne's physical and emotional development.

....

....

....

....

....

....

....

....

....

....

....

....

....

....

....

....

....

....

....

10 marks

Total for Question 1 = 30 marks

Revision Guide
pages 6 and 14

Hint

For this **evaluate** question you need to consider different aspects of Leanne's likely physical and emotional development. It is important to give both positive and negative ways in which Leanne may develop.

Prepare

Before you begin your answer, you could plan your writing by compiling bullet lists of negatives and positives. As you write, you can tick them off.

Prepare

By revising, and completing practice papers, you will start to be able to answer questions without writing bullet lists. Remember, you will have limited time in the actual assessment.

Hint

Think about the ways in which physical improvements might influence Leanne's emotional development.

Hint

You need to finish your answer with a conclusion, saying whether the overall likely impact will be positive or negative.

Revision Guide
page 21

Hint

For this **identify** question you simply have to find the facts asked for using the information provided on the graph.

Hint

To find the answers, you need to identify the correct vertical bar and read the percentage of tumours on the vertical axis (the y axis). You can do this most accurately by placing your ruler horizontally on the graph, with its side touching the end of the relevant bar. The percentage shown on the point where the ruler crosses the vertical axis is the answer.

Explore

Practise looking at other graphs, so you can get used to finding information.

2 | Leanne's grandmother, Sally, died at the age of 45 from cancer of the womb and Clare was diagnosed with the same cancer last year at the age of 43.

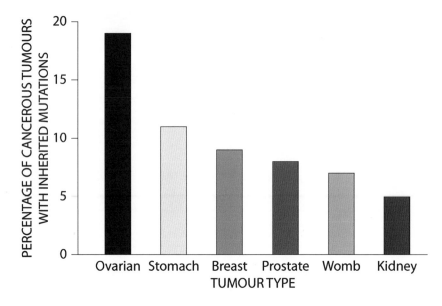

(a) Using the data shown in the graph, identify:

(i) which type of tumour shows evidence of the highest percentage of inherited mutations

....

....

(ii) the percentage of womb tumours that show evidence of inherited mutations.

....

....

2 marks

(b) To what extent might the knowledge of her grandmother dying of womb cancer, and her mother now being diagnosed with womb cancer, affect Leanne's emotional wellbeing?

....

....

....

....

....

....

....

4 marks

Revision Guide pages 14, 20, 21, 29 and 30

Hint

For this **to what extent** question you need to state clearly the reasons which support your overall view or opinion.

Hint

You are only required to write about Leanne's emotional wellbeing (not her physical, intellectual or social wellbeing).

Hint

The effects will mainly be negative but you may be able to think of a positive effect.

Hint

Your answer should finish with a conclusion. Note that there may be a positive effect, but the effects will mainly be negative.

Explore

Certain factors can increase the risk of developing womb cancer, such as obesity, diabetes and age.

Revision Guide
page 25

Hint

For this **describe** question you need to identify possible effects and then add some detail. For example, if Leanne was upset she may have been unable to concentrate at school.

Prepare

Look back at the information given about the family to find out how old Leanne was when her parents divorced, and anything else that happened when her parents split up.

Hint

Your answer should include two effects, which can be one positive and one negative, or two positives, or two negatives.

Hint

You can consider short-term effects on **different** aspects of Leanne's development – think about physical, intellectual, emotional and social needs (PIES) when planning your answer.

(c) Describe **two** of the possible short-term effects on Leanne's development of her parents divorcing when she was a child.

1 ....

....

....

2 ....

....

....

4 marks

(d) To what extent does the unpredictable life event of looking after a close family member who has developed a life-threatening illness affect someone's health and wellbeing?

....

....

....

....

....

....

....

....

....

....

....

....

....

....

....

....

....

....

....

....

....

....

....

....

`10 marks`

Revision Guide
pages 29 and 30

Hint

For this **to what extent** question you need to consider all effects on someone's health and wellbeing of looking after a close family member who has a life-threatening illness.

Prepare

Remember that there will be positive effects of looking after the family member as well as negative, so it is important to include some of each. Before you begin your answer, write down your initial ideas – you could list the negatives and positives in two columns.

Hint

You should include positive and negative points covering physical, intellectual, emotional and social needs (PIES) to make sure you give a balanced answer and reduce the risk of repeating the same point.

Hint

This is a general question, so you do not have to relate your answer to any of the individuals mentioned in the case study material in this practice assessment.

Hint

Finish with a conclusion which gives your opinion as to the overall effect, depending on the balance of positive and negative answers you have included.

Revision Guide
pages 27 and 37

Hint

For this **evaluate** question, you need to consider both positive and negative effects on health and wellbeing.

Hint

You can include examples from different religions if it helps to explain what you mean.

 Prepare

To help you plan your writing, note down your initial thoughts and ideas – you could then add an N or a P next to each one to indicate whether it's negative or positive.

Hint

Your first paragraph could describe the negative aspects and your second paragraph could focus on the positive aspects.

Hint

Finally, finish with a conclusion which gives your overall opinion, based on the balance of your answers.

Watch out!

The information mentions Peter converting to a different religion, but the question is a general one rather than about Peter. It also asks about converting at **any** life stage. This means you do not need to write about Peter. You can include factors such as contraception in your answer as the question is not only about later adulthood.

Peter has recently started taking more of an interest in spiritual matters and has decided to convert to a different religion after long conversations with an old friend.

(e) Evaluate how converting to a new religion may affect an individual's health and wellbeing at any stage of adulthood.

....

....

....

....

....

....

....

....

....

....

....

....

....

....

....

....

....

....

....

....

10 marks

Total for Question 2 = 30 marks

3 (a) To what extent will being at nursery impact on Ben's social development?

....

....

....

....

....

....

....

....

4 marks

Revision Guide
pages 16 and 17

Hint

For this **to what extent** question you need to state clearly the reasons to support your overall view or opinion.

Hint

Look back at the information given earlier in this practice assessment to remind yourself of Ben's age. Don't be tempted to guess – be sure to check!

Hint

Your answer must focus on **social** development. You won't gain any marks by writing about any impacts on Ben's physical, intellectual or emotional development.

Revision Guide
page 16

Hint

For this **explain** question you need to state the three different types of relationships and add some detail about who they form between.

Hint

If you can't remember the three different types of relationships, think about yourself in school or college and at home. Which three different groups (or types) of people do you have relationships with?

As Ben passes through the life stages to early adulthood he will develop relationships with others in different situations.

(b) Explain the **three** different types of relationships.

1 ....

....

....

2 ....

....

....

3 ....

....

....

6 marks

Peter has always been fit and active but has started to lose his sight. This is why he has moved in with Leanne, Dave and Ben.

(c) Evaluate how the degeneration of Peter's sight is likely to affect his health and wellbeing.

....

....

....

....

....

....

....

....

....

....

....

....

....

....

....

....

....

....

....

....

....

....

....

10 marks

Revision Guide
page 33

Hint

For this **evaluate** question include some effects of Peter's degenerating eyesight on his physical, intellectual, emotional and social needs to give a more balanced answer.

Hint

Although losing his sight will have a negative effect on Peter's health and wellbeing, there are ways he can regain some of his independence. You should include some positive points as well as the negative effects.

Hint

You could start your answer with a first paragraph about ways in which losing his sight will affect Peter in a negative way, as it will be easier to think of those.

Hint

Your second paragraph could start with a phrase like 'However, there will be ways in which Peter can enjoy a happy life despite losing his sight...'. Then go on to describe some positives.

Hint

Finish with your conclusion about how, overall, Peter's health and wellbeing will be affected by the deterioration in his sight.

Revision Guide
page 37

Hint

For this **evaluate** question think about what you have learned about the **psychological** effects of ageing to consider how Peter's health and wellbeing will be affected as he gets older. Remember to read back though earlier information to remind yourself what you have already been told about Peter.

Hint

Structure your answer by writing a paragraph saying how moving in with his family may affect Peter, and then writing about changes that will happen as he gets older and how those may affect him. Finish with a conclusion saying how you feel Peter will be affected overall.

Hint

The examples you give must show that you understand how psychological effects of ageing will affect Peter. Remember that there will be some positive effects as well as negative, so you should include those in your answer.

Hint

The question does not ask you to include theories of ageing, but it is acceptable to refer to these if you wish, when thinking about how changes in his life may affect Peter socially.

(d) With reference to the psychological effects of ageing, evaluate how different changes in his life, other than losing his eyesight, are likely to affect Peter's health and wellbeing as he ages.

....

....

....

....

....

....

....

....

....

....

....

....

....

....

....

....

....

....

....

....

....

| 10 marks |

| Total for Question 3 = 30 marks |

| **TOTAL FOR PAPER = 90 MARKS** |

Practice assessment 4

Answer ALL questions.
Write your answers in the spaces provided.

1 Margaret is 62 years old and her husband, Ian, is 74 years old. They have a son, Craig, who is 32 years old and married to Debbie. Craig and Debbie have two children, Lucy who is 6 years old and Jack who is 2 years old. Margaret and Ian also have a daughter, Sarah, who is 30 years old and recently divorced.

(a) Identify **two** developmental milestones Jack will have passed through as he acquires his language skills.

1 ....

....

2 ....

....

2 marks

Revision Guide
pages 2 and 12

Time it!

Time yourself completing this practice assessment. Aim to complete it in 90 minutes. Try to leave yourself a little time to check your answers once you have finished the paper. Remember that the actual time allowed for your assessment might vary, so check the latest guidance on the Pearson website to be sure you are up to date.

Hint

In this **identify** question you need to simply state the required facts – so here you need to write down two developmental milestones that a child aged 2 will have passed through.

LEARN IT!

A **milestone** is an ability achieved by most children by a certain age.

Revision Guide
pages 5, 6 and
7

Hint

To answer this **identify** question you need to state the life stage which a person meeting developmental norms would be passing through when each of these physical changes happened to their bodies. You don't need to add any further explanation.

Time it!

This **identify** question is only worth 4 marks so don't take too much time by writing more than you need to. Aim to spend no more than 4 minutes writing and checking your answer.

LEARN IT!

A **developmental norm** is a description of an average set of expectations with respect to a person's development.

(b) Identify which life stage Margaret will most probably have been passing through when she experienced:

(i) puberty

....

....

(ii) pregnancy and lactation

....

....

(iii) perimenopause

....

....

(iv) menopause.

....

....

4 marks

Revision Guide
page 14

Sarah has a negative self-esteem and self-image, despite having had a happy family life, and being told by her parents throughout her childhood and adolescence how pretty she is. Margaret and Ian found out when she was in her early twenties that Sarah had been bullied at school, being called names and isolated by the more popular girls in her year group because she was pretty, well behaved and intelligent.

(c) Explain the difference between self-image and self-esteem.

....

....

....

....

....

....

....

....

4 marks

Hint

The command word **explain**, and the marks available, mean that for the **two** aspects of self-concept asked about you need to:

- say what each means
- give an example for each to show you understand the definition.

Hint

Your examples can be ones from the information about Sarah or ones of your own.

Revision Guide
page 18

Hint

The command word **describe**, and the number of marks available, mean that you need to:

- write about the **two** main points you pick, and

- the **two** ways in which critics say Gesell's theory does not work.

Hint

You could structure your answer by writing two paragraphs.

- You could start your first paragraph with 'Gesell said that...'. Following with 'He also said that...'.

- Your second paragraph could start with 'His critics say that...'. Then you could follow that with 'His critics also say that...'.

(d) Describe the difference between two of the main points of Gesell's maturation theory and what his critics suggested was wrong with his theory.

....

....

....

....

....

....

....

....

4 marks

Revision Guide
page 19

Lucy is in Year 1 at school and has been in trouble recently for being cheeky. She does this to make her classmates laugh. Craig and his wife, Debbie, are concerned, so they make an appointment to see the teacher about her behaviour. The teacher tells them that Lucy has been copying her friend Poppy's behaviour. They ask that Lucy be moved to sit with a different group of children. They also set up a reward chart at home for when the teacher writes in her school planner that Lucy has behaved that day. This works and she behaves well again in school.

(e) Explain why social learning theory suggests how Lucy learns to behave.

....

....

....

....

....

....

....

....

....

....

....

6 marks

Hint

For this **explain** question you need to mention each of the four stages of Bandura's social learning theory and apply them to Lucy's actions and behaviour.

Time it!

This question is worth 6 marks so it should take you no longer than 6 minutes, including time to read and check what you have written and to amend it if necessary.

LEARN IT!

Social learning theory suggests that the way children behave is an interaction between personal and environmental factors.

Revision Guide
pages 16, 17
and 26

Hint

For this **evaluate** question you need to consider different aspects, both positive and negative, of Sarah's likely social and intellectual development.

Prepare

Before you begin to write, you could compile two bullet lists which include positive and negative ways in which Sarah may develop socially and intellectually. You can tick them off to make sure you have covered all of them in your answer.

Hint

Don't be tempted to include points linked to emotional development – you won't gain any marks for them.

Time it!

An evaluate question can take quite a long time to answer but try to avoid spending too long on it. Aim to spend no longer than 9 minutes writing your answer and then a minute quickly checking it.

Although Sarah was verbally and emotionally bullied at school, she ignored the bullies as much as she could and never retaliated. She had a small group of very close friends who were very similar to her. Although her parents were unaware of the bullying situation, she was always loved, encouraged and given every opportunity to learn and mix with others out of school. She did well at school, despite the bullying.

(f) Evaluate the likely impact of Sarah's experiences at school on her social and intellectual development.

....

....

....

....

....

....

....

....

....

....

....

....

....

....

....

....

....

....

....

....

....

....

....

....

....

10 marks

Total for Question 1 = 30 marks

Hint

Finish with a conclusion, saying whether the overall likely impact will be positive or negative, based on the answers you've given.

Watch out!

Although you already know from Question 1 (c) that Sarah has a negative self-esteem, this does not necessarily mean that her social and intellectual development will have been negatively affected.

Revision Guide
page 22

Hint

This **identify** question requires you to simply state the answers you work out from the chart. You don't need to add any detail.

Hint

The chart shows how the foetus develops during pregnancy. The darker areas represent times when the alcohol damage to the foetus is at its greatest. The lighter areas represent times when potential harm exists but the risk is slightly reduced.

Explore

FAS is caused by exposure to alcohol in the womb: it is strongly recommended that alcohol should be avoided altogether during pregnancy.

2   Craig has a child, Olivia, from a previous relationship with Sophie. They moved in together when they were both 18 years old and partied a lot, drinking heavily. They were unaware that Sophie was expecting a baby until she was 8 weeks pregnant. Olivia was born with foetal alcohol syndrome (FAS). Craig and Sophie split up after two years, due to Sophie blaming herself for Olivia's FAS and Craig feeling Sophie should have suspected she was pregnant sooner.

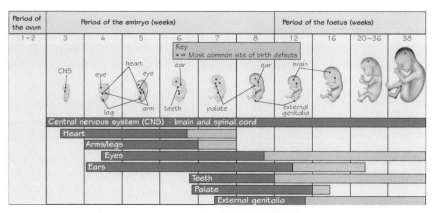

The possible effects of drinking alcohol during pregnancy at various stages of development of the embryo/foetus

(a) Using the data shown in the chart, identify:

(i)   during which weeks the embryo's arms and legs are most at risk of damage if alcohol is consumed by the mother.

....

....

(ii) which part of the embryo/foetus is most at risk of harm for the longest time if the mother consumes alcohol.

....

....

2 marks

(b) To what extent might FAS affect Olivia's growth and development?

....

....

....

....

....

....

....

....

4 marks

Revision Guide
page 22

Hint

For this **to what extent** question you need to state some of the likely effects of FAS on Olivia's growth and development. You then need to give a brief conclusion stating the overall likely effect on Olivia.

Hint

Your answer needs to focus on Olivia's **physical** development.

 Time it!

This type of question can take too much time if you describe the effects in detail instead of just stating them. Try to keep your answer concise and spend no more than 4 minutes answering and checking your answer.

Revision Guide
page 14

Prepare

Before you begin to write your answer, you could compile a bullet list of possible effects. In your answer you just need to describe them briefly.

Hint

For this **describe** question you need to identify possible effects on Sophie's emotional wellbeing and then add some detail, such as 'She will have a negative self-esteem because she feels it is her fault.'

Hint

Don't be tempted to let your answer stray into talking about the effects on Olivia; remember that the question focuses on Sophie.

(c) Describe the possible effects on Sophie's emotional wellbeing, knowing that her drinking caused Olivia to have FAS.

....

....

....

....

....

....

....

....

4 marks

Revision Guide
pages 23 and
29

Margaret and Ian are worried about Sarah, who asked her husband for a divorce because she no longer loved him. Although Sarah knows it was the right thing to do, she and her ex-husband have had to sell the house to split their finances and she has moved into a modern flat with no garden. She is unhappy living on her own.

(d) To what extent is Sarah's divorce likely to affect her health and wellbeing?

....

....

....

....

....

....

....

....

....

....

....

....

....

....

....

....

....

....

....

....

10 marks

Hint

Remember that there will be both positive and negative effects of divorcing, so it is important to include some of each.

Prepare

Before you begin to write, you could draw two spider diagrams – one for positive effects and one for negative effects. You can tick them off when you are writing to make sure you have covered all the points you want to make.

Hint

Be sure to cover a mixture of physical, intellectual, emotional and social needs so that your answer will be more balanced and you will be less likely to have repeated any point.

Hint

In this **to what extent** question you need to finish with a conclusion. This should give your opinion as to the overall effect on Sarah's health and wellbeing depending on the balance of positive and negative answers you have included.

Revision Guide
pages 28, 29
and 30

Hint

For this **evaluate** question you need to consider both positive and negative effects. You then need to finish with a conclusion in which you give your overall opinion, based on the effects you have identified.

Prepare

Underline or highlight any relevant information you have been given in any of the case study information; this will help you to think of possible effects of Craig's redundancy on the children's growth and development.

Hint

To gain a high mark you need to include a good range of effects and finish with your overall opinion.

Watch out!

The question asks you about the children's growth and development so each point you make must be relevant to that. For example, if you write about Craig and Debbie's relationship suffering you must say how that might affect the growth and development of the children.

Craig is unexpectedly made redundant. Although he is confident that he will get a new job this proves to be harder than he first thought. As a result, Debbie has to take a job as a teaching assistant while Craig looks after Jack all day and collects Lucy after school. They now have a lot less money available to them. Although Margaret and Ian offer to help out in any way they can, Craig's pride stops him accepting any financial support.

(e) Evaluate how Craig's redundancy may affect the growth and development of his children, Lucy and Jack.

....

....

....

....

....

....

....

....

....

....

....

....

....

....

....

....

....

....

10 marks

Total for Question 2 = 30 marks

3 Margaret's mother, Laura, is 88 years old. She is slim, and generally fit and healthy, although she has osteoarthritis, which is slowly worsening. She lives on her own in a house about three miles away from Margaret.

(a) To what extent will having osteoarthritis affect Laura physically, now and in future years?

....

....

....

....

....

....

....

....

4 marks

Revision Guide
page 34

Hint

For this **to what extent** question you need to state clearly and concisely several different effects of Laura's osteoarthritis.

Hint

Finish with your overall view or opinion. For example, what might the physical effects of arthritis lead to Laura needing, and would this affect her positively or negatively overall?

Watch out!

To gain high marks you are only required to assess the physical effects of Laura's osteoarthritis. You won't gain anything by writing about emotional or social impacts.

Revision Guide
page 34

Hint

For this **explain** question you need to state what things Alf will be missing from his diet and then describe the physical effect each one will have on Alf.

Hint

An example of a specific dietary lack could be iron – a shortage of this could lead to anaemia.

Watch out!

Water and fibre are essential and should be included in your answer but be careful to use the correct terminology. Water and fibre are not nutrients so shouldn't be referred to as such.

Laura's husband, Alf, died three years ago. He had had a stroke which left him paralysed down one side and without speech; when he left hospital, he moved to a nearby nursing home. He found it increasingly hard to swallow so ate and drank less and less. He eventually died of organ failure a few months after his stroke.

(b) Explain the likely physical effects on Alf of not eating and drinking enough.

....

....

....

....

....

....

....

....

....

....

....

....

6 marks

Revision Guide
page 36

Ian has had prostate cancer for the past 10 years, but it has now spread to his bones. Although it is being controlled by medication, he has started to feel more pain, look much older and show the first signs of dementia.

(c) Evaluate how the degeneration of Ian's health is likely to affect other areas of his development.

....

....

....

....

....

....

....

....

....

....

....

....

....

....

....

....

....

....

....

....

....

10 marks

Hint

For this **evaluate** question you need to include several different ways Ian's development will be affected and explain how these will affect him overall.

Hint

Try to include some effects on Ian's physical, intellectual, emotional and social development to give a more balanced answer.

Hint

Try to include positive effects if you can – how might Ian's relationships be affected?

Hint

Finish with a conclusion in which you give your overall opinion as to how Ian's illness will affect his development and quality of life.

Time it!

Remember that you are aiming to complete this assessment in 90 minutes. This question should therefore take you a maximum of 10 minutes. Make sure you spend part of that time reading through your answer to check you haven't made any mistakes.

Revision Guide
pages 39 and
40

Hint

For this **evaluate** question you need to think about what you have learned about the impact of an ageing population and give several effects of this.

Hint

You need to include some positive points to show you have considered all aspects of the issue.

Hint

Remember that all the effects you state must be linked to the UK **economy**. So, for example, increasing numbers of older people needing healthcare services leads to higher costs.

Hint

Finish with a conclusion giving your overall opinion on how the UK's economy is being affected by an ageing population. Base your conclusion on the balance of the points you have included in your answer.

LEARN IT!

The **old-age dependency ratio** is the ratio of people older than 65 (so assumed to be retired) to the number of people of working age. Working age is defined as being between 15 and 64.

Life expectancy in the UK has increased and the birth rate has fallen. This means that there are now more people in later adulthood in the UK. The old-age dependency ratio has risen.

(d) Evaluate the economic effects of an ageing population in the UK.

....

....

....

....

....

....

....

....

....

....

....

....

....

....

....

....

....

....

....

....

....

....

....

10 marks

Total for Question 3 = 30 marks

TOTAL FOR PAPER = 90 MARKS

Answers

Use this section to check your answers.

- Definitive answers are provided for questions with clear and correct answers. Where a question has an alternative correct answer, this is also provided.
- Where the answers to some questions are individual or require longer responses, bullet points show the key points you could include in your answer or how your answer could be structured. For these questions, your answers should be written using sentences and paragraphs and you might include some but not necessarily all of the points.

Practice assessment 1

(pages 1 to 15)

1 Primary characteristics are processes that are related to the sex organs present at birth, and these characteristics start the maturation process when sex hormones are released.
Your answer should include two examples from the following:
- menstruation begins
- uterus and vagina grow
- ovulation occurs.

Secondary characteristics are not necessary for reproduction, and these develop when sex hormones are released.
Your answer should include two examples from the following:
- growth of armpit and pubic hair
- increased layers of fat under the skin
- breasts enlarge
- growth spurt
- hips widen.

2 Emily's rate of growth will slow down.

3 Your answer may include examples from the following:
- Belle is asking lots of questions to satisfy her curiosity.
- Her memory is developing so she can talk about things past or anticipate things that may happen in the future.
- She is starting to read and write words and sentences of increasing difficulty.
- She is starting to draw in detail.
- She is learning not to use incorrect forms of words, such as 'I five' instead of 'I am five'.
- She is using words such as 'first', 'next' and 'then' when telling a story.

4 In your answer you should start by outlining Piaget's theory. Next, you need to talk about how Lucas will develop an understanding or concept about something, called a schema, and, then, how his experience will fit with this schema. When he has a new experience that disturbs the schema his understanding will change to take account of the new experience, so developing a new schema.

Example content about his experience of crawling may include:
- Piaget's theory explains how children use their experiences to construct their understanding of the world around them.
- As Lucas crawls he learns about his environment.
- He may crawl on something soft like a carpet and develop a schema about the floor.
- His experience in various rooms fits with this schema.
- As he develops in confidence and crawls further he may then crawl into the kitchen and the floor will feel different, which upsets his schema.

- He will change his schema to accommodate his new experience of the surface he is crawling on, so will develop a new schema.

Alternative answers:
Crawling can teach Lucas a lot about his environment, so you could write about, for example, the contrast between crawling on something soft or hard, rough or slippery, solid or viscous, hot or cold, bumping into soft or hard things, etc.

5 In your evaluation, you should:
- demonstrate through the quality of your answer that you have accurate and thorough knowledge and depth of understanding of the definition, and the theories, of attachment
- show that you can link the various factors to reach an overall judgement as to how well Lucas's attachments develop during the infancy stage
- give a well-balanced, logical and clear evaluation, showing an awareness of both positive and negative points, leading to a conclusion
- use the correct language, such as 'attachment', write fluently and pay attention to spelling and grammar.

Example content may include:
- Attachment is the emotional bond that is formed between infants and their main caregiver.
- Bowlby's theory is that infants have an inbuilt need to form an attachment to a carer.
- The quality of this attachment will affect emotional development, and so the ability to form positive relationships, for the rest of the child's life.
- Schaffer and Emerson's stages of attachment show that Lucas will have responded to any caregiver during the first 3 months of his life.
- Between 4 and 7 months he will have shown a preference for Samantha, his primary caregiver, but accepted care from others.
- Between 7 and 9 months he preferred Samantha and sought comfort from her, being unhappy when separated from her and fearful of strangers.
- From his current age, 10 months, he will show distress when Samantha first leaves him and resist contact when she returns, according to Ainsworth's Strange Situation classification (SSC).
- He will now begin to form attachments with others who respond to him, so will be starting to form an attachment to Natalie, who he is already used to accepting care from.
- By 18 months he will have formed attachments with all those who look after him.

Conclusion:
- Because he has formed a secure attachment to Samantha, his main caregiver, he will grow up with the emotional resources needed to cope with uncertainty in life and to build positive relationships.

6 In your discussion you should:
- show that you have accurate and thorough knowledge and understanding of the facts, making sure that you include most of the answers given below
- give a well-balanced, logical and clear argument, including both positive and negative points, leading to a conclusion which is supported by the evidence given in the scenario
- take care with spelling, grammar and the correct use of any specialist terms, such as 'genetic predisposition'.

Example content may include:

Genetic:
- Robert's father died of a heart attack.
- His mother has high blood pressure.

- His mother is of South Asian origin.
- There is a possibility of genetic predisposition.

Lifestyle choices:
- Robert takes part in extreme swimming.
- He does a lot of travelling.
- He is up very early to fit in training.
- He competes in races and is always trying to beat his own time.
- He has an unbalanced diet – eats a lot; snacks on biscuits; enjoys takeaway meals.

Combined:
Robert's heart attack could have been caused by:
- an inherited condition
- stress due to: balancing work, training and family life; competition; his diet; or being pre-diabetic.

Conclusion:
- You must include a conclusion to your discussion which says what combined factors might have led to his heart attack.

7 In your evaluation you should:
- show that you have accurate and thorough knowledge and understanding of the facts, making sure that you include most of the answers given below
- link all the various aspects of Robert's health issues to the development of the rest of the family
- give a well-balanced, logical and clear argument, including both positive and negative points, ending with a conclusion which is supported by the evidence given in the scenario
- take care with spelling, grammar and the appropriate use of any specialist terms, such as 'attachment'.

Example content may include:

Positive:
- Robert is at home recovering, so he will spend more time with the family, which may make them happier.
- The home atmosphere will be less stressful now Robert isn't rushing off racing, or to train or work.
- When he is on the road to recovery, Robert will be able to look after Lucas, so Samantha will not have to rush to get him ready to take with her on the school run. This will give her more time to talk to Emily and Belle before leaving the house in the morning, and to Belle on her journey to and from school. This will help Samantha and her two oldest children feel better about themselves (Samantha because she feels less guilty about not giving each child enough attention, the children because they are getting more attention).
- Robert is at home so Lucas will develop a strong attachment to him more quickly.
- All the family will have a better diet, as there will be no more takeaways and sugary snacks in the house, reducing the risk of obesity and developing better habits for later in life.
- The children will have more chance to talk to Robert and may learn from him.
- Robert will be less stressed as he is not working, so there will be a more relaxed atmosphere at home and all will be happier.
- Samantha will enjoy having Robert at home at the weekend instead of off racing, so their relationship may become stronger.
- While Robert is not swimming, the family might have more money to pay for trips out, so helping their social and intellectual development.
- They may accompany Robert on his walks, so become fitter.

Negative:
- Robert may become irritable and bored due to inactivity, so make the rest of the family unhappy.
- Samantha will have more to do now she is looking after Robert and taking him to his various appointments as he recovers, so may have less time for the children.

- Emily will be expected to help out more with her siblings and in the house, which may affect her social life.
- Emily may have less time for her homework, so this could affect her intellectual development.
- Emily may become resentful of her father.
- The children may be anxious about their father and become scared of losing him or Samantha, making them clingy.
- Once Samantha returns to work and Robert is feeling better he can do some of the childcare and chores, so reducing Samantha's stress.

Conclusion:
- You need to finish your evaluation with a statement of how you think Robert's issues will affect the development of the rest of the family overall, based on the facts you have included in your answer. For example, you might say that on balance you feel that Robert's issues may help the development of the rest of the family as he will be at home more often so spending more time with his family.

8 Remember that Emily is 12 and at the early stages of puberty. You will need to make at least six separate points.

Example content may include:

Negative effects:
- Emily may not be able to have the things she wants for a while (new phone, clothes, trainers), so may become resentful and less able to concentrate at school.
- They may not be able to afford items Emily needs for school, so may buy cheaper uniform, etc, which will embarrass Emily so affect her concentration.
- They may not be able to afford for her to go on school visits, so she may miss out on new learning opportunities.
- They may not be able to afford extras such as music lessons, so she will have fewer chances to learn new skills.
- Emily may fall in with the wrong crowd, because she is resentful and rebellious, and skip some lessons or school.
- Robert and Samantha may be more stressed at home, so less likely to spend time encouraging or helping Emily to complete her homework. Emily may take advantage of this to go into her bedroom and spend the evening on her phone instead.

Positive effects:
- Emily may spend more time with her grandmother after school, who is there looking after Lucas, so learn different things or see things from a different point of view after chatting with her.
- Samantha has to go to work to make some money, so Emily will see more of her father. He may be better at subjects that Samantha was less good at, so be better able to help her with her homework.
- Emily may decide to try extra hard at school to make her parents proud, to support her parents through this difficult time.
- She may go out for walks with Robert and learn about what they pass, such as nature.

9 Your answer should include at least six separate effects on Samantha's emotional health.

Example answers:
- She will enjoy feeling that she is part of something other than her family, so has an additional role in life.
- She will enjoy making new friends and having more opportunities to interact socially with other adults.
- She may feel guilty that she is enjoying being away from her family.
- She may miss Lucas, who she has not left before, despite enjoying work.
- She may enjoy the mental stimulation and new challenges that work brings her, so her self-esteem may increase.
- She may worry about how her mother is coping with Lucas.

10 Your answer may include examples from the following:
- GP services, such as providing medication
- counselling
- memory clinic
- support in the home with personal care, such as home help, meals on wheels or district nurse.

11 In your answer you should:
- show that you have accurate and thorough knowledge and understanding of the relevant information
- show that you can link the various factors to reach an overall judgement as to how Fred's life changes will affect his social wellbeing
- give a well-balanced, logical and clear argument, giving both positive and negative points, leading to a conclusion which is supported by the evidence given in the scenario
- use any technical language and terms, such as 'Alzheimer's disease' and 'socially isolated', correctly, consistently and fluently, paying attention to spelling and grammar.

Example content may include:

Positive:
- Fred being able to return home after his stroke, so he is able to spend more time with Joan and the other members of his family.
- Fred having a family to spend time with, now Joan is ill.
- Fred not drinking to excess so he doesn't suffer from hangovers, so is better able to socialise when family and friends call round.
- He still has a garden so he can easily chat to neighbours.

Negative:
- Fred and Joan had to move from their own house into sheltered accommodation, so Fred misses old friends and neighbours, who may be unable to travel to see them because of their age and reduced mobility.
- Fred's own health issues – stroke – make it harder to socialise as he can't drive.
- Reduced mobility reduces Fred's physical ability, so he is unable to play bowls, which could lead to reduced social contact.
- A loss of shared hobbies with Joan and friends – crosswords, TV quizzes, pub quiz – so Fred misses their chats.
- Joan's health issues take up a lot of his and the family's time, so there is less time to enjoy a chat.
- There may be negative effects of drinking alcohol on his own; he may feel isolated and lonely.
- There may be negative effects of smoking if visitors don't like the smell or passive smoking.
- Fred not being able to go to the pub with his friend any more as he feels he should stay at home with Joan.

Impact on social wellbeing:
- Fred was able to resume social life on return home from hospital.
- Fred enjoyed his friend picking him up as it gave him a chance to socialise with other friends at the pub.
- Fred may miss being able to drive, as this may result in reduced opportunities for socialising as it's harder to get out.
- He now has more responsibility so he feels he shouldn't go out.
- Fred is unable to go to the pub, he misses his friends and the pub quiz, and there are fewer opportunities to socialise now.
- He enjoys chats with neighbours, but this is not the same as seeing his friends in the pub.
- He may lose confidence to chat to others as he is seeing fewer people.
- There is less chance to have a meaningful conversation with Joan as her condition worsens, and they are no longer able to discuss crosswords and TV quizzes.
- He misses Joan's company as her memory fails, and they are no longer able to do crosswords and watch TV quizzes together.

- Samantha helps, but she's in a hurry with not much time to chat.
- Fred is able to enjoy a drink, but it is on his own, which makes him feel lonely and socially isolated.
- His smoking may put friends and family off calling.

Conclusion:
- This will depend on the balance of your answer, but you might write that, overall, recent life changes will have led to a deterioration in Fred's social wellbeing.

12 Your answer could include two examples from the following:
- taking on the role of looking after Joan
- taking on the role of looking after the house and garden
- joining the exercise class
- giving up smoking.

Suggested explanations could include:
- Activity theory says that older people:
  o don't show a decline in interest in life and don't want to become isolated
  o have the same social and psychological needs as those of younger people, so they adjust to the ageing process, that is changes in health and mobility, by taking on new roles and hobbies.
- He wants to improve his mobility and does this by joining an exercise class and through this he meets new friends, so is less socially isolated.
- Through the class he loses some weight, which will help his fitness, so he will be better able to look after Joan and fulfil his new role in life.
- Giving up smoking will help him become fitter to take on the jobs Joan used to do to run the home.
- By giving up smoking and becoming fitter and more mobile he will live longer, so will be around to look after Joan and fulfil his role for longer.

13 In your answer you should:
- show that you have accurate and thorough knowledge and understanding of the possible effects of smoking on health and wellbeing
- show that you can link the various factors to reach an overall judgement as to how Fred giving up smoking will affect his health and wellbeing
- give a well-balanced, logical and clear argument, giving both positive and negative points, leading to a conclusion which is supported by the evidence given in the scenario
- consistently use the correct language, so refer to cigarettes, not 'cigs' or 'fags', write fluently and pay attention to spelling and grammar.

Example content may include:
- Fred's skin, breath, hair and clothes won't smell of smoke, so his personal hygiene will improve.
- Fred's peak flow reading will improve so he will be less breathless when he exerts himself.
- Fred will reduce the risk of developing diseases such as lung cancer.
- Fred may find it harder to concentrate at first as he will be craving a cigarette.
- Fred may be irritable as he will miss having a cigarette.
- Fred's mood may improve, as he will feel better about himself by giving up a habit he knows his family dislikes and that he knows is bad for him.
- Fred will be happier because he will be able to exercise better when he is less breathless.
- Fred will be aware that the house will smell better for Joan and the rest of his family, so will feel pleased with himself.
- Fred may become more stressed about his home situation as he cannot use cigarettes to relax.
- Fred will have more energy as he can breathe better.

- Fred's appetite will improve.
- Friends and family who do not like visiting the home of a smoker may be more likely to call round to see Fred and Joan, so Fred will be happier and feel more supported.

Conclusion:
- Fred's health and wellbeing will improve overall as there are many more positive than negative results of giving up smoking.

Practice assessment 2

(pages 16 to 29)

1 (a) Your answer should include two examples from the following:
- menstruation (periods) stops
- hot flushes
- night sweats
- loss of libido
- mood swings
- vaginal dryness.

(b) Your answer should include the two facts given below:
- During parallel play children play next to each other with their own set of toys and may copy each other but they don't interact.
- In cooperative play children share toys and play together. They interact.

(c) Your answer could include two of the points below, or other relevant answers of your own.

Sean may find that:
- he loses muscle tone and strength if he exercises less
- he puts weight on, as he may eat the same amount of food as he did when he was younger but may become less active
- he starts to lose height due to changes in posture and compression of the spinal discs and joints
- his hair starts to thin due to changes in hormones
- his vision becomes less sharp due to cataracts starting to develop or age-related macular degeneration
- his hearing becomes less sharp due to a build up of wax or damage to the ear due to age
- his touch becomes less sensitive due to a decrease in the number of receptor cells
- his food will taste more bland as the number of taste buds decreases
- his ability to smell will decrease due to a decrease in the number of sense cells in the nose.

(d) Example answers include the following:
- They will have been able to use simple sentences with some mistakes, such as 'I saw two mans' when they were aged 5, but will now be able to use more complex sentences, such as: 'I saw two men walking along the road today.'
- They will have been able to ask questions and see things from their own perspective at the age of 5, but by 8 years old they can use simple logic so can reason to solve simple problems.

(e) Your answer should include at least six of the facts given here, all due to the increase in testosterone:
- penis enlarges
- prostate gland will produce secretions
- testes enlarge and produce sperm
- facial hair grows
- spontaneous erections and ejaculation
- hair grows in armpit, chest and pubic area
- muscles will increase
- growth spurt
- voice box grows causing the voice to deepen (break).

(f) Example content may include:

Positive:
- There may be clubs and teams she can join to get more exercise.

- There will be new learning opportunities.
- Some of Mollie's friends from school may be there so this will help her become more confident at college.
- There will be new opportunities to interact with others and make new friends.
- Mollie may enjoy the additional freedom of being at college rather than school.
- She may be influenced by her new friends to take part in sport, study harder, eat more healthily or exercise more.
- She will learn more about her own abilities.
- Mollie will take more responsibility for her own actions.
- Mollie may become more independent and have a more positive self-concept.
- She may form a more serious intimate relationship and become more contented and secure.

Negative:
- Mollie may be influenced by new friends to make poor lifestyle choices, such as smoking, drinking, drugs, unprotected sex or unhealthy diet.
- She may find it hard to make new friends so feel isolated.
- She may miss her old school friends if they go to a different college so be unhappy.
- Mollie may find the work too hard so have negative self-esteem.
- She may find the work boring, or too easy, and be tempted to truant with her new friends.
- Mollie may compare herself with others and find herself lacking in some way, which may have a negative effect on her self-esteem and self-image.
- She could be bullied, which may affect her self-confidence and ability to learn.

(g) Example content may include:
- Caitlyn will have been particularly busy between the twins being born and starting school so may have seen mainly family members. She may have had limited opportunity to mix with others socially. She will now be spending time with her work colleagues so will make new friends.
- Caitlyn will dress more smartly and take more care with her appearance now she is back at work, so her self-image will become more positive and she will be more confident when meeting and mixing with new people such as clients.
- Although she loves her children, Caitlyn will enjoy the change of scene and the sense of freedom when she is away from the family and will feel as though she has a purpose in life other than being a wife and mother, or stepmother.
- She will be learning new skills, so her self-esteem will improve.
- She will have fun with her new friends but will miss and appreciate her family more, so will be happier when she returns home.
- She may find working and looking after the family and home hard work, so may become tired and irritable.
- If she gains promotion she will enjoy her new status and responsibilities.
- She will need to use her reasoning, decision-making and communication skills, so will feel happy that she is challenging herself intellectually.

2 (a) Your answer should include at least three points from each of the nature and nurture answers given here.

Example content may include:

Nature:
- Children inherit physical characteristics from their parents.
- Children inherit skills and abilities from their parents.
- Children form attachments with their primary caregivers.
- Children may have a genetic disposition.

Nurture:
- Children learn through play and their environment.
- Children learn behaviours from their environment.
- Children learn and develop skills and abilities at home and school.
- If children are neglected in the first three years of their lives they find it much harder to form strong relationships later in life, with possible consequences including anxiety, depression, learning difficulties or delinquency.
- A child's environment and life experiences can trigger a genetic disposition.

(b) Your answer should include nine different effects, including some short-term and some long-term effects, and finish with a conclusion.

Example content may include:

Short-term effects:
- stress or anxiety
- low self-esteem
- poor self-image
- unable to concentrate on work at school
- reluctant to join in activities where they may come to the notice of the bullies
- become withdrawn or isolated
- physical harm if physical bullying.

Long-term effects:
- eating disorders
- self-harm
- substance abuse
- poor academic achievement
- difficulties in forming relationships
- poor mental health
- increased risk of suicide.

Conclusion:
- Bullying is likely to have a long-term effect on the development of a child unless tackled straight away.

3 (a) Your answer should include at least six points, some positive and some negative, from the list given here or other relevant answers of your own.

Example content may include:

Positive:
- Martha has a close relationship with Tavi as she spends so much time with him.
- She is happy looking after Tavi in such a nice home and area.
- Martha may have a chance while Tavi is resting each day to do the housework, develop her creative skills or take an online course.
- She will enjoy taking Tavi out in the fresh air when the weather is good enough, and will get fresh air and exercise herself.

Negative:
- Martha may have a bad back from the strain of lifting Tavi.
- She may have developed health problems from the strain, such as heart conditions, high blood pressure, digestive problems or headaches.
- She may become resentful of staying at home all day and be irritable with the rest of the family.
- Martha will miss Bethia's help when she is away at university and have to do more herself.
- Martha may not have had as much time as she would have liked to help Bethia when she was growing up.
- Bethia may resent the time spent with Tavi and this could affect her relationship with Martha, causing Martha to be unhappy.
- Bethia may have had more freedom than usual when she was an adolescent as Martha was so busy, so Bethia may have made some poor lifestyle choices, causing Martha anxiety or stress.

- Martha may not have looked after herself, maybe putting on weight and not taking care with her appearance, which could lead to poor self-image, and this could affect her relationship with Adlai.
- Martha may miss going to work and feel she has lost her skills.
- She may not have many opportunities to meet with friends or new people so may be socially isolated.
- She may feel lonely during the day when Tavi is resting.
- Martha may not sleep very well at night worrying about Tavi or listening in case Tavi needs help.
- Tavi may get frustrated and take it out on Martha, causing her distress, or even physical harm.
- Martha may find it stressful having to take Tavi for medical appointments.
- Access to health and social care services may be made harder, so more stressful for Martha, by them living in a village.

(b) Your answer could include at least three positive and three negative answers from the list below or other relevant answers of your own.

Example content may include:

Positive:
- Bethia may enjoy spending time with her parents again.
- She may enjoy helping with Tavi and feeling she is contributing after her parents have supported her through university.
- She may enjoy living at home again, without having to study or do everything for herself.
- Bethia may value input from her parents when she is writing letters of application.
- Bethia may enjoy spending time at home more than before she left for university now that she has spent time away and has realised how much she missed her home and family.

Negative:
- Bethia may resent the fact that she is now home with spare time on her hands but is expected to help with Tavi, and she will then feel guilty that she feels like that.
- She may get bored and feel isolated now she is back in the village.
- She may find it hard living at home after living away and having the freedom of not having to think about the effects of her actions on the family.
- Bethia loves her brother but feels sad that he can't have the life she has because of his disability.
- She may be affected by her parents' stress and worry about Tavi.
- Bethia may feel frustrated that she is back home when she thought she would leave university and move into a job and a place of her own, earning her own money.
- She may feel worried about not having a job yet and uncertain about what the future holds.

(c) Your answer could include at least three positive and three negative answers from the list below or other relevant answers of your own.

Example content may include:

Positive:
- Bethia will earn her own money and so will be able to afford to eat healthily, exercise, go on holiday and get a place to live.
- Her job will allow her to use and improve her skills and knowledge.
- Her self-esteem will improve as she will feel she has not let herself or her parents down and is proud of her achievement and status.
- She will meet new people and make new friends.

Negative:
- Bethia may find it hard to afford a place of her own and everything else she needs at first to set up on her own.

- She may worry that she will find the intellectual demands of the job hard at first and may doubt her own ability, and worry about what others think of her, so her self-image may become more negative.
- She will be living on her own, maybe in a different part of the country, so may be sad as she misses her family and friends.
- Bethia may feel socially isolated at first, until she makes new friends through her job and any local clubs that she decides to join to help her meet people.

Conclusion:
- Overall getting a job will have a positive effect on Bethia's health and wellbeing, as the negative points will only be temporary as she first moves and starts the job.

(d) Your answer could include at least nine answers from the list below, or other relevant answers of your own.

Example content may include:

Positive:
- Tavi will be proud of his sister and happy for her.
- Tavi will have his parents all to himself again so will be happy about that.
- Tavi will look forward to her visits home.

Negative:
- Tavi will miss his sister, so be sad when he thinks about her.
- He may resent the fact that she is able to have a full and active life when he has to live at home.
- He may worry about what will happen to him when his parents die and Bethia has a job in another part of the country.
- Tavi will have one less person to chat to and have a laugh with, so will be more isolated again.
- He will worry that his mother does so much more for him now that Bethia isn't there to help out and do some of the tasks.
- He will miss being able to discuss things with Bethia and stretch himself intellectually.
- He will miss the company of a young person, close to his own age.

Conclusion:
- Conclude whether the overall effect on Tavi will be positive or negative, depending on the balance of the answers you have given.

4 (a) Your answer should include at least six of the points below or other relevant answers of your own.

Example content may include:

Positive:
- He may sometimes enjoy the freedom of not having to think about what Barbara wants to do or eat. For example, he will now have total control of the television so may enjoy watching what he wants with no complaints from Barbara.

Negative:
- Arthur still grieves for her and misses her every day, so often feels very sad.
- He feels less safe and secure, so may suffer from problems such as high blood pressure, headaches, anxiety and sleeplessness.
- He may not always eat as healthily as he used to, eating more ready meals.
- He has no-one to sit close to, or sleep with, on a daily basis any more, so misses that intimacy and familiarity.
- He has no-one to chat to, or just be with, on a daily basis, so feels lonely and isolated.
- Arthur has no-one to chat to other than neighbours in the sheltered accommodation and his family when they visit, so he may feel that his world has shrunk, and that he has less to say or to challenge him intellectually.

- Arthur has lost his identity as part of a couple, so feels lost without Barbara.
- He can't get used to being on his own and having to make day-to-day decisions on his own, so has feelings of self-doubt and negative self-image, self-esteem and self-concept.
- Arthur feels less confident without her.
- He may feel stressed and prefer to die than live on alone.

(b) Your answer should include a statement of each theory, and at least four examples to support each theory, from the list provided here, or other relevant answers of your own.

Example content may include:

Activity theory says that people have the same social and psychological needs throughout their lives so need activity and social interventions whatever their age, adjusting to their declining health, mobility and strength but still wanting to join in within their own limitations.

Support services could help Arthur with this in a variety of ways (you need to include at least four in your answer):
- The warden at the sheltered accommodation will, or should, be arranging activities to provide the residents with activity and social interventions, so could visit Arthur regularly to tell him what is happening and when, and encourage him to join in.
- The warden could invite Arthur to be on an events committee and encourage him to contribute his ideas about activities that could be organised, so he not only socialises more but uses his brain more.
- The occupational health services will come and make sure he is capable of cooking himself a meal or ironing his clothes. They will also supply any aids he needs.
- Hospital transport service will pick him up and take him back home if his doctor refers him for any health problems he has as a result of his age and the stress of losing Barbara.
- Volunteer visitors from voluntary groups, such as charities, could provide more regular company for Arthur, so he has someone to chat to and to take him to, or encourage him to join in with, any events being run locally.
- Social services can arrange for him to be picked up and taken to a day centre regularly, so he can take part in activities and socialise with others of his own age.

Social disengagement theory says that people naturally withdraw from social contact in older age, and society withdraws from them, so they tend to focus on their previous life and activities. Because their families expect less of them they become more dependent, and, with the right support, can become tranquil and happy.

Support services could help Arthur with this in a variety of ways (you need to include at least four in your answer):
- His doctor can give him medication for any medical issues that arise from his bereavement, such as sleeplessness and headaches, and refer him to other services to help him cope with his grief.
- A bereavement counsellor could help Arthur learn to cope with his grief.
- Social services can arrange for him to be picked up and taken to a day centre regularly, so he can talk or reminisce about his earlier life and engage in activities with people of his own age.
- Various charities offer volunteer visitors who could visit Arthur occasionally to help him with practical tasks, such as shopping.
- If Arthur has a religious faith, someone from his church could visit him to talk about Barbara and help him cope with his grief.
- Meals on wheels services can deliver meals to him, so he is eating a balanced, healthy diet.

Practice assessment 3

(pages 30 to 44)

1 (a) Your answer should include the fine motor skill given below and either one of the examples listed here or a relevant answer of your own.

Ben will be developing the tripod grasp. This will enable him to:
- use a fork and spoon
- turn pages of a book
- button and unbutton clothing
- use a pencil to copy letters
- build a tower of cubes.

(b) Your answer should include four of the following or other relevant answers of your own:
- starting nursery
- starting school
- going through puberty or some aspect of male puberty such as voice breaking
- moving to high school
- meeting his first girlfriend or boyfriend
- moving to college or university
- getting a job.

(c) Your answer should include two of the following for each child:
- Ben will show distress when Leanne leaves him.
- Ben will go to Leanne for comfort when upset.
- Ben will be happy with strangers when Leanne is present.
- Ben will greet Leanne when she returns.
- Ollie will not show distress when his mother leaves.
- Ollie will continue to explore his environment when his mother leaves him.
- Ollie may go to a stranger for comfort.
- Ollie may show no interest in his mother when she returns.

(d) Your answer should include at least four of the points given below: two about what Piaget believed and two about what his critics believe.

Example content may include:

Piaget believed that:
- children pass through distinct developmental stages in sequence
- children should be allowed to discover things for themselves through spontaneous play
- children can only see things from their own perspective until they are 7 years old.

His critics believe that:
- Piaget underestimated children's rate of development
- with support children can develop more advanced concepts sooner than Piaget suggested
- children can be given experiences that help them to move through the stages of development at a faster rate
- some children can see things from the perspective of others before the age of 7.

(e) Your answer should include at least six of the facts below, and should include at least one from each of middle and later adulthood.
- Dave has now acquired expert knowledge about the practical aspects of life.
- He applies the knowledge, skills and experiences he has gained so far in his life.
- This helps him think logically and make judgements about important matters.
- His thinking becomes realistic and pragmatic.
- His job role will require him to think through problems and make decisions, sometimes about complex situations.
- New brain cells will still be developing at his current age of 25 and as he gets older.

- In middle adulthood there may be a gradual decline in the speed at which he processes information, although he will still be developing new brain cells.
- In later adulthood he may take longer to learn and recall information, but his brain will still be producing new brain cells.
- How effectively his brain continues to work in later adulthood will depend on his lifestyle and daily activities.

(f) Your answer should include at least nine of the points below and be a mixture of both positive and negative points, and it should finish with a conclusion.

Example content may include:

Positive:
- Her weight may decrease, and her body will become more toned.
- Her stamina may improve and become even better than when she was younger.
- Her flexibility may improve and become even better than when she was younger.
- Her strength may improve and become even better than when she was younger.
- Her fertility could increase as her weight goes down.
- She could feel happy because she is starting to do something other than looking after the needs of her family.
- She could feel happy about her improved personal appearance due to her weight loss and toned body.
- She could compare herself more favourably with others once she feels better about herself.
- She could feel more confident as she becomes fitter and leaner.
- The exercise will release endorphins which could trigger positive feelings and a positive outlook on life.
- The exercise could help her sleep and reduce any stress she is feeling.
- Her self-image and self-esteem, and so her self-concept, could become more positive.
- She could feel more attractive to her husband again.

Negative:
- She may feel guilty using the time Ben is at nursery to exercise instead of doing jobs at home.
- She may feel guilty leaving Dave and Peter to babysit while she goes to her dance classes.
- At first, she may find it harder than expected, and may even be discouraged from continuing.
- She may find it so much harder because she is tired and heavier so have negative self-esteem.
- She may compare herself with others she sees running or at the dance classes and find herself lacking in some way, which may have a negative effect on her self-esteem and self-image.

Conclusion:
- The overall impact will be positive as she is likely to quickly start to regain her fitness and see many more positive benefits.

2 (a) (i) Ovarian

(ii) 7%

(b) Your answer should include at least four of the different effects below, or other relevant answers of your own, and should finish with a conclusion.

Example content may include:
- She may worry that she has a genetic disposition towards womb cancer.
- She will be worried about herself and will feel guilty for doing so because her mother is the one who is already ill.
- She may worry that because she has put on weight she has increased her risk of developing womb cancer.

- She may become stressed and anxious thinking that she is going to die and the effects this will have on her family, especially Ben.
- She may want to have another child and decide to do this soon, so she can then tackle the possible risk of womb cancer.
- She may become determined to reduce the risk by having a hysterectomy before womb cancer can develop.
- She may become depressed wondering why this is happening to her.
- She may develop negative self-esteem.
- She may be grateful that at least she knows there is a disposition towards womb cancer in the family, so she can do something about making sure it doesn't happen to her.

Conclusion:
- Leanne is likely to worry at first and then tackle the problem.

or
- Leanne is likely to worry without taking any action, which will negatively affect her emotional wellbeing.

(c) Your answer should include two points from the list below, or other relevant answers of your own.

Example content may include:

Negative:
- She will probably have been upset that she was no longer able to see her father as often, especially after he moved to a different part of the country.
- She may have been unable to concentrate on work at school so her intellectual development may have been negatively affected.
- Money may have been a problem, so she might not have been able to have the things she used to have so felt resentful.
- She may have become withdrawn and this could have affected her social development.
- She may have had trouble sleeping due to anxiety. This would have affected all aspects of her development as she would have been tired, and so become run down and more likely to be ill.
- They may have had to move to a smaller house in a worse area, which would have embarrassed her.

Positive:
- She may have developed a closer relationship with her mother.
- She may have been glad that her parents split up if they were arguing all the time, so be happier.
- She may not have got on very well with her father and be relieved he had left.
- She may have been able to concentrate better at school once the stress of living with parents who argued all the time had gone, so her intellectual development may have been positively affected.

(d) Your answer should include at least nine points, some positive and some negative, from the list below, or other relevant answers of your own, and finish with a conclusion.

Example content may include:

Positive:
- The person may develop a closer and stronger relationship with the family member because they are supporting them through illness.
- They may learn more about the relative (and other family history if an older family member) if they are spending more time talking to them.
- They may enjoy having someone to spend time with, especially if the person would otherwise be on their own in the house.

Negative:
- They may be distressed and worried about the family member being ill.

- They may feel resentful of spending time looking after them and feel guilty about feeling like that.
- Other younger family members may have more freedom than usual while another family member is looking after the relative, so may make some poor lifestyle choices, causing extra anxiety or stress.
- They may feel a loss of some independence when someone else is reliant on them.
- They may have less time for exercise.
- They may have less time for learning opportunities.
- They may not have many opportunities to meet with friends or new people, so may become socially isolated.
- They may develop health problems from the stress, such as heart conditions, high blood pressure, digestive problems or headaches.
- They may get frustrated and take it out on other family members, causing distress.

Conclusion:
- Overall the health and wellbeing of the person looking after the family member will be negatively affected.

(e) Your answer should include at least nine points, including both positive and negative answers, from the list below, or other relevant answers of your own. You should finish with a conclusion, stating your own overall opinion depending on the balance of your answers.

Example content may include:

Positive:
- The individual may have to follow dietary restrictions that lead to a better, more balanced diet which lowers the risk of high cholesterol, heart diseases and high blood pressure, so he or she becomes more healthy and lives longer.
- There may be periods of fasting, such as Muslims do during Ramadan, leading to a loss of weight for the individual, reduced cholesterol levels and a whole-body detoxification.
- The individual may find contentment and peace when worshipping.
- They may be more positive about death because they are comforted by thought of an afterlife.
- They may follow safer sexual practices, so there is less risk of sexually transmitted conditions.
- They may have stricter rules about cleanliness, so there is less risk of illness transmitted by touch.
- The individual may make new friends through attending a place of worship.
- The individual will learn about a new religion, so have an extra learning opportunity.
- They will feel valued by others who hold the same beliefs.
- They will feel supported and accepted by others who hold the same beliefs.

Negative:
- There may be dietary restrictions, such as Buddhist and Hindus being vegetarian. These could lead to deficiencies in nutrients needed to maintain a healthy body and brain.
- There may be periods of fasting, which could lead to risks such as heartburn, malnourishment and dehydration and make existing health conditions worse.
- The religion may have restrictions on medical treatments, such as Jehovah's witnesses not having blood transfusions, or some Buddhists being reluctant to take certain medicines, preferring to use alternative therapies, which could lead to a deterioration in health and even death.
- There may be restrictions around family planning, which could lead to unwanted pregnancies and births.
- There may be restrictions around abortions, which could lead to unwanted births.

- The religion may have specific requirements for after death, such as being buried before nightfall, which could cause distress to other family members of other faiths who want to take more time preparing to say goodbye.
- The religion may have restrictions on organ transplantation, leading to death.
- The individual may be discriminated against or excluded because of their new beliefs.
- The individual may be upset when their beliefs are not understood.

Conclusion:
- Converting to a different religion will affect an individual's health and wellbeing positively overall as the contentment and reassurance will outweigh any negative outcomes.

3 (a) Your answer should include at least four answers from the list below, or other relevant answers of your own.
- Ben may start to develop special friendships.
- He may feel socially secure and confident because he is making friends.
- He may become more independent.
- He is likely to start to develop relationships with peers and adults.
- Ben will probably learn that behaving well gives him satisfaction when he is praised, so he is likely to behave in a way that is socially acceptable.
- He should learn to play cooperatively, so he won't have temper tantrums if he doesn't get his own way.
- Ben is likely to play with other children, share toys and take turns.
- He is likely to develop his communication skills and start to appreciate the feelings of other children.
- Ben may be influenced to behave badly by copying the behaviour of some other children, but overall being at nursery should have a positive impact on Ben's social development.

(b) Your answer should include the three different types of relationships given below, along with some detail as to who they form between.
- Formal relationships – do not involve emotional attachment and develop between non-related individuals such as colleagues, or teacher and learner, and help to develop positive self-esteem and self-image.
- Informal relationships – develop within family and with significant people in a person's life, and prepare for the building of other informal, formal and intimate relationships throughout life by promoting positive self-concept.
- Intimate relationships – develop between two people who are physically attracted to each other and lead to contentment, emotional security and positive self-image.

(c) Your answer should include at least nine of the points below, including both positive (if you can think of any) and negative points, or other relevant answers of your own. You should finish with your overall opinion (conclusion), based on the balance of the answers you have included.

Example content may include:

Positive:
- He will be able to apply to have a guide dog as there is no upper age limit, so will still be able to maintain some independence.
- He could listen to talking books so can still enjoy a book independently and continue to learn from books.
- His family could help rebuild his self-confidence by talking to him and working out solutions together, and praising the progress he makes.

- His family and friends can help him by asking what he needs them to do and being available to him, so he will feel less helpless and isolated.
- Others can start conversations with him by saying, for example, 'Hello Peter, it's Dave here,' so he always knows who is in the room with him, so he feels less isolated.
- There are rehabilitation services available to help him learn to live with his new disability and give him living skills training, so he can do practical tasks for himself and maintain some independence.
- His house can be adapted to make the home environment safer and more functional for him, for example making sure there are no trip hazards by keeping furniture in the same position and spaces between clutter free.

Negative:
- He may have reduced opportunities for socialising as he will eventually not be able to drive any more and will also find it difficult travelling on public transport.
- He will feel less safe, secure or confident, so may suffer from problems such as high blood pressure, headaches, anxiety and sleeplessness.
- He may feel lonely and isolated when the family are out.
- He might not be able to get used to losing his sight so may develop negative self-image, self-esteem and self-concept.
- He is likely to be upset by his loss of independence.
- He may become depressed after being fit and active for so long.
- He could be anxious in new situations as he won't be able to see what is happening around him.
- He may struggle to take part in leisure activities such as reading, bowling and walking around in a new environment.
- He could find it harder to join in conversations as he won't know who is standing or sitting where, so could feel isolated in company.

Conclusion:
- Although overall losing his sight will have a negative effect on Peter's health and wellbeing, he should start to adapt and regain some of his independence.

(d) Your answer should include at least nine different psychological effects of ageing, and how they are affecting Peter's health and wellbeing, using examples from the list below, or other relevant answers of your own. Finish with a conclusion saying how he will be affected overall as he gets older.

Example content may include:

Positive:

Peter may:
- find his new religious beliefs help, as he will feel part of that community so less isolated
- enjoy his leisure time as he finds new activities to keep his brain occupied and his body active
- be more content as he has wisdom and has reached a stage in his life where he is happy with his family and what he has achieved in life, and doesn't feel the need to strive for anything else
- have worried about retiring because of a lack of purpose but has increased leisure time to enjoy the company of his granddaughter and great grandchild
- have lost his home but will enjoy spending more time with his family
- enjoy new social interactions in his new neighbourhood if he wants them and continue to involve himself in the community while adjusting to his declining health, mobility and strength (activity theory).

Negative:

Peter may:

- still be grieving the loss of his wife but will have come to terms with it after 20 years and has his family and friends for company
- find it harder meeting his friends as his sense organs degenerate, leading to depression and other mental health conditions
- become more aware of his own mortality as his circle of friends becomes smaller as they die
- feel helpless and no longer useful as his reliance on his family increases and he loses his independence, so his self-esteem will become more negative
- become increasingly anxious about whatever he faces each day as it starts to take him longer to process information
- lack confidence and give up more easily as he finds it harder to complete daily tasks on his own
- feel marginalised by society as he feels less worthy as he no longer has the status he once enjoyed in his working life
- find it difficult to adjust to no longer being the head of the family, the provider and decision-maker, but instead is living with his granddaughter, and his family are taking over many of these functions
- prefer to withdraw from some social contact as he ages and focus on his previous life and activities (his family can help him by talking about their memories of family life with him (social disengagement theory)).

Conclusion:

- Although Peter is coping at the moment, social change could bring about a sense of loss, anxiety, reduced confidence and lower self-esteem as he ages, although this is likely to be reduced by the support of his family.

Practice assessment 4

(pages 45 to 60)

1 (a) Your answer should include two of the following, or other relevant answers of your own:
- using gurgling and crying to communicate, for example when needing food or comfort
- saying a few words
- linking two or three words together.

(b)

(i) Adolescence

(ii) Early adulthood

(iii) Early adulthood

(iv) Middle adulthood.

(c) Your answer should include the two definitions below and an example of each, or other relevant answers of your own.
- Self-image is how individuals view themselves and is influenced by how they feel they are perceived by others.
- For example, an attractive person may think of themselves as plain or ugly because they have been told that in early childhood and/or adolescence.
- Self-esteem is how individuals value and feel about themselves.
- For example, a person with a positive self-esteem will have an optimistic view of the world and life in general so will expect things to go well for them, while a person with a negative self-esteem will expect things to go wrong for them.

(d) In your answer you should include two of the points below from Gesell's maturation theory and the two points made by his critics.

- Gesell said that development is a predetermined biological process and that the environment has little influence.
- Gesell said that children follow the same orderly sequence in their development.
- Gesell said that the pace of development may vary depending on physical and intellectual development.
- Critics say that his theory does not explain individual or cultural differences.
- Critics say that his theory does not help explain the development of children with learning difficulties.

(e) Your answer should include the six points below.
- Lucy likes and admires Poppy and sees her getting her classmates laughing when she is cheeky (vicarious reinforcement).
- Lucy has observed and remembered how Poppy behaves.
- Lucy thinks about this and copies Poppy's behaviour the next time she has the opportunity.
- Lucy is told off by the teacher and her parents, which she doesn't like (negative reinforcement).
- Lucy enjoys the personal satisfaction of being praised (intrinsic reinforcement) or the rewards (extrinsic reinforcement) she earns through behaving (positive reinforcement).
- Lucy is motivated to stop the poor behaviour.

> While your answer should use what is in Bandura's theory, you don't need to mention Bandura explicitly, which means you would not gain a mark for stating the words 'Bandura's theory' but you would gain marks for showing how to apply the theory to the situation.

(f) Possible answers should include at least nine of the points below, or other relevant answers of your own, but must be a mixture of both positive and negative points. You also need a conclusion saying whether the impact is likely to be positive or negative overall.

Example content may include:

Positive:
- Her friendships will be very close, which will help her develop stronger relationships in the future.
- She will have learned who to trust by her experiences with her friends and the group of bullies.
- Her family will have helped her develop socially by giving her opportunities to mix with others out of school.
- She will have become even closer to her family, feeling relieved and safe at home.
- She will have developed mental strength by ignoring the bullies and doing well despite the bullying.
- She had friends who were very similar to herself so will not have been persuaded by peer pressure to truant, miss lessons or engage in any other risky behaviour.

Negative:
- She will have felt isolated at school if she had to attend classes or events without her small group of friends.
- She may have made sure she was in sets with her friends by, for example, doing less well in PE to get in a group away from the bullies, so affecting her grades some years.
- She may have found it harder to concentrate when she was in a group with any of the bullies, which could have affected her intellectual development, so although she did well, it's possible she could have done even better.
- She may have been reluctant to speak up in class when she was in a group with any of the bullies, because, whether she got an answer right or wrong, she was worried about what they would say. This could have been viewed negatively by her teachers and affected her grades in subjects such as languages.

- She may find it harder to trust others as an adult and may tend to remain closer to her family than other people.

Conclusion:

- The overall impact on her social and intellectual development will be positive as she will make new friends as she moves through adulthood based on her positive experience with her own group of school friends. She is likely to have a good job due to her academic abilities, so will meet people similar to herself and continue to have new work challenges and learning opportunities.

2 (a)

(i) During the fourth, fifth and sixth weeks of pregnancy.

(ii) Central nervous system.

(b) Your answer should include at least four effects from the list below, but only one of each type of effect, finishing with a conclusion about the likely overall effect on Olivia.

She may have:

- a small head circumference
- neurological problems due to damage to the central nervous system (brain and spinal cord), for example learning difficulties; poor organisation; lack of inhibition; difficulty writing or drawing; attention problems or hyperactivity
- abnormal growth, so smaller than expected norms
- development delay, so learning difficulties
- facial abnormalities, for example small and narrow eyes; small head; smooth area between nose and lips; or thin upper lip
- health problems, for example heart defects.

Conclusion:

- FAS is likely to affect Olivia's size and development throughout her life, due to Sophie drinking for the first 8 weeks when the embryo was first developing.

(c) Your answer should include at least four points from the list below or other relevant answers of your own.

Example content may include:

- She will feel guilty, which will affect her moods.
- She will worry about Olivia's attitude towards her when she finds out that her problems are due to her mother's drinking.
- She may become withdrawn because she devotes all her time to looking after Olivia.
- She might have trouble sleeping due to anxiety caused by her guilt, so become drained and find it even harder to cope emotionally.
- She will resent Craig for seeming to blame her and not standing by her, so may find it hard to trust other men.
- She will have negative self-esteem as she will feel bad about herself.
- She will have a negative self-image as she will think that others will feel badly about her because of what she has done.
- She may suffer additional guilt if she ever feels irritated or annoyed with Olivia when she can't do or understand something due to her condition.

(d) Your answer should include at least nine points, giving some positive and negative, from the list given here, or other relevant answers of your own. Finish with a conclusion which gives your opinion as to the overall effect depending on the balance of positive and negative answers you have included.

Likely effects could include:

Positive:

- Sarah is happier now she is not living with someone she doesn't love.
- Sarah is happy and excited at first as she feels as though she has a fresh start.
- She is relieved she has finally reached a decision.
- She will enjoy a sense of freedom and regain her independence.

- Sarah has less work to do looking after a flat rather than a house and garden.

Negative:

- Sarah feels sad that their marriage has broken down.
- She feels guilty about how her decision has affected her husband.
- Sarah feels as though she has failed, so may be depressed.
- She may be unhappy that she no longer has a garden or somewhere to sit on nice days and get some fresh air.
- Sarah feels isolated as she can't chat to neighbours when she is out in the garden as she used to be able to.
- Sarah feels stressed about her finances, so may have difficulty sleeping.
- She may be unhappy about living on her own after being used to living with her family and then her husband.
- She has to do everything for herself now, including all the paperwork and finances, so may have less opportunity for leisure activities, for example exercise, and learning opportunities.
- Sarah may not be able to afford luxuries like holidays now she is setting up on her own again.
- She may have lost some of her friends who were joint friends.
- She may feel unable to take up some social opportunities now she is single again and most of her friends are in couples.
- Sarah may develop health problems from the stress, such as high blood pressure, digestive problems and headaches.
- She may get frustrated and take it out on other family members, causing distress.

Conclusion:

- Overall Sarah's health and wellbeing will be negatively affected until she starts to meet new people and gets used to living on her own in her flat.

(e) Your answer should include at least some positive points and a total of at least nine overall, either from the list below or other relevant answers of your own. Finish with a conclusion, giving your overall opinion depending on the balance of your answers.

Example content may include:

Positive:

- Jack, in particular, will spend more time with Craig, and Lucy will see more of Craig after school before Debbie comes home from work, so the children will enjoy developing a stronger relationship with their father.
- Jack may get more chance to do things like play with Craig and develop skills like kicking and throwing a ball, so improving his motor skills.
- Jack will spend more time with Craig now, so may learn different things from him and do different free activities with him than he did with Debbie.

Negative:

- Jack will miss spending time with his mother and he could show distress when she leaves and resist contact with her when she returns, so affecting their relationship.
- They may not be able to afford for Lucy to take part in extracurricular activities such as clubs for which there is any charge, so she will have fewer opportunities to mix with others, so affecting her social development.
- Lucy may not be able to take part in extracurricular physical events, such as sporting or dancing, for which there is a charge, so may miss opportunities to develop her motor skills.
- Lucy will feel as though she is missing out if she cannot have what her school friends get, such as new trainers and clothes, so may be embarrassed or resentful and become withdrawn, possibly losing friends and slowing her social development.
- Lucy may feel too embarrassed to invite her friends to her home if they can no longer afford treats such as fast food.

- The family may not be able to afford such healthy food, so the children's physical development might be adversely affected.
- Craig may feel he is a failure and become depressed, resentful or moody, so leading to arguments with Debbie, which may have negative effects on the children's development. For example, Lucy may not be able to concentrate at school because she is worried about her parents arguing.
- Craig will feel guilty that he is not able to provide for his family like he used to, so will be stressed and may lose his temper with the children; this could cause them distress, feelings of a lack of security or regression such as Lucy bed-wetting and Jack misbehaving.

Conclusion:
- Overall Craig's redundancy will negatively affect the children's growth and development until he gets a new job or lets his parents help them out.

3 (a) Your answer should include at least four points from the list below, or other relevant answers of your own, including the statement at the end about needing a stick and a stair lift.
  - Laura will have swelling and pain in her joints.
  - There may be damage to the soft tissue around her joints.
  - Laura may have difficulty walking.
  - Laura may have difficulty climbing stairs.

Therefore, Laura is likely to have to walk with a stick and eventually need a stair lift.

(b) Your answer should include six of the points listed below or other relevant answers of your own.

Example content may include:
- His body will have become less efficient at absorbing nutrients due to the ageing process, so he will now be at greater risk of malnutrition.
- He will be absorbing fewer essential nutrients, such as:
  o vitamin D, which is essential for absorbing calcium, so he will suffer bone loss
  o vitamin B12, so his red blood cells will be created more slowly and his nerve function will reduce
  o vitamin C, so the healing and the development of healthy tissue in his body will slow down
  o calcium, so he will have more bone loss and increased risk of fracture and osteoarthritis
  o magnesium, so he will have a less efficient immune system and reduced heart function
  o potassium, so his bones will be weaker, and he will have reduced cell and kidney function
  o iron, so he will be more at risk of developing anaemia
  o omega-3, so he will be more at risk of developing rheumatoid arthritis and macular degeneration
  o proteins, so his body won't be able to repair cells
  o fats, so he will have less energy for bodily functions
  o carbohydrates and sugars, so he will have less energy for bodily functions.
- He will be absorbing:
  o less fibre, so his digestion will become less efficient, which means he may become constipated
  o less water, so he will have an increased risk of dehydration, which may cause damage to his organs and digestive system.

(c) Your answer should include at least nine of the points below, or other relevant answers of your own, and should finish with a conclusion which gives your overall opinion, based on the answers you have included.

Example content may include:
- His body will be less able to fight infections such as coughs, colds and pneumonia.
- He will have less stamina.
- His mobility will become reduced.

- He will be in pain and discomfort.
- His senses will become less sharp.
- His short-term memory will deteriorate.
- He will find it harder to make decisions.
- His reactions will slow down.
- His verbal communication will deteriorate as his ability to respond and react to information slows down.
- He may have less opportunity to socialise with others because he is ill or in pain.
- He may have reduced ability to socialise with others as his ability to communicate deteriorates.
- He will be distressed if he becomes incontinent or less able to communicate with others.
- He will feel as though he is losing his independence or control of his life when he can no longer do tasks such as see to his personal care, so will be upset.
- He will have lower self-esteem, self-image and self-concept.
- He may feel closer to his family as they all help and support him.

Conclusion:
- The degeneration of his health will affect all aspects of his development, mainly in a negative way.

(d) Your answer should include at least nine different economic effects, either from the list provided below, or other relevant answers of your own. Finish with a conclusion which states your overall view on how the UK's economy is being affected by the ageing population overall.

Example content may include:

Effects include increased costs due to:
- a rise in the number of older people needing access to health and social services which keep them healthy, leading to a good quality of life and longer independence, which will mean more services are required
- a rise in the number of older people with chronic conditions who need to use health and social services, which will mean more services are required
- a rise in the number of people being eligible for a state pension, so more money being taken out of the national pot, which will mean less money for economic investment
- advances in medicine mean that more people are living longer, again needing more services
- families becoming less willing, or unable, to care for older family members at home, so more care homes are needed
- a rise in the number of older people in the UK who like to be active in their retirement, so more services, other than health and social care and sheltered accommodation, are needed to meet their leisure needs
- increased taxes to pay for these additional needs.

Other effects include:
- A rise in the number of older people staying in their own homes for longer as they live longer, so fewer larger homes are available for young families to buy.
- Fewer people to replace older people when they retire due to the falling birth rate so a shortage of skilled workers.
- Some older people staying on at work longer meaning that fewer jobs are available for younger people.
- A rise in the number of older people staying active in their retirement, so there are more people available to do volunteer work which helps the economy of organisations such as charities.
- The government raising the retirement age, so people will have to work longer to meet the increased costs via taxes.

Conclusion:
- Overall, the number of people of working age who support the needs of older people is becoming fewer, which will keep increasing the pressure on the UK's economy.

Printed in Great Britain
by Amazon

23657408R00046